TWAYNE'S WORLD AUTHORS SERIES

A Survey of the World's Literature

Sylvia E. Bowman, Indiana University
GENERAL EDITOR

SPAIN

Gerald Wade, Vanderbilt University
EDITOR

Carlos Arniches

(TWAS 188)

TWAYNE'S WORLD AUTHORS SERIES (TWAS)

The purpose of TWAS is to survey the major writers—novelists, dramatists, historians, poets, philosophers, and critics—of the nations of the world. Among the national literatures covered are those of Australia, Canada, China, Eastern Europe, France, Germany, Greece, India, Italy, Japan, Latin America, the Netherlands, New Zealand, Poland, Russia, Scandinavia, Spain, and the African nations, as well as Hebrew, Yiddish, and Latin Classical literatures. This survey is complemented by Twayne's United States Authors Series and English Authors Series.

The intent of each volume in these series is to present a critical-analytical study of the works of the writer; to include biographical and historical material that may be necessary for understanding, appreciation, and critical appraisal of the writer; and to present all material in clear, concise English—but not to vitiate the scholarly content of the work by doing so.

Carlos Arniches

By DOUGLAS R. McKAY

*University of Colorado
at Colorado Springs*

Twayne Publishers, Inc.   : :   New York

To Diane

Preface

Carlos Arniches (1866–1943) is a key figure in the development of the modern Spanish theater. Best known to his countrymen as "The Illustrious *Sainetero*," he contributed more than any author of his day to the rise and splendor of the so-called *género chico,* that festive satellite of stage drama which delighted audiences for over thirty years with comical one-act depictions of the language, customs, and sentiments of everyday life. With the creation of the grotesque tragedy, in which he intermingled elements of the comic and the tragic, the sportive and the serious, Arniches advanced to a rank of respected leadership as one of the masters of twentieth-century Spanish drama.

His total production amounted to 191 plays, the majority of them written in collaboration.[1] I have selected for discussion only those titles which have best magnified the playwright's prestige and are most exemplary of the evolution and literary distinction of his theater. Understandably, in the large repertory of Arniches' plays we find several insignificant *sainetes, zarzuelas,* and melodramatic farces which are unworthy of serious critical evaluation.[2] These writings add little by way of artistic credit to Arniches' reputation. In this connection, I have endeavored to indicate in the appendix which are the best and the least good of the author's writings. No attempt has been made to comment upon the fascinating topic of Madrid's dialect in Arniches' plays, a subject which, while of great interest to students of his theater and to readers of the Spanish language, must remain outside the context of the present study.[3]

I express my appreciation to the personnel at Norlin Library, University of Colorado, for making available from their special holdings of García Rico y Cía's *Colección de comedias españolas de los siglos XIX y XX (Collection of Spanish Plays of the 19th and 20th Centuries),* amounting to 3,763 plays written between 1800 and 1941, a large portion of Arniches' 124 coauthored plays. In addition, E.M. del Portillo's four-volume compilation of the sixty-seven plays Arniches wrote unaided has also served as my primary source, from which a number of quotations have been taken. The English translations of titles, quoted material, and two of Arniches' sainetes are my own.

I am grateful to Vicente Ramos and Manfred Lentzen for the clear and penetrating ideas they put forth in their respective critical biographies of Arniches, to which mention has been made in my text and bibliography. My sincere thanks go also to Professors Edwin Honig of Brown University, for permission to quote from his introduction to *Miguel de Cervantes: Interludes,* and Gerald E. Wade of Vanderbilt, for his helpful suggestions and kind encouragement.

Materially, the preparation for this study was aided by a grant-in-aid from the University of Colorado's Council on Research and Creative Work, for whose generosity I hereby express appreciation.

DOUGLAS R. MCKAY

University of Colorado at Colorado Springs

Contents

Chronology

1866   October 11: Arniches born in Alicante.

1880   Moves to Barcelona with his family.

1885   His literary ambitions take him to Madrid.

1887   He publishes his first nondramatic work, *Cartilla y cuaderno de lectura (Reading Primer)*.

1888   February 9: Première of his first play, *Casa Editorial (Publishing House)*, written in collaboration with Gonzalo Cantó.

1890   November 25: *Nuestra señora (Our Wife)*, his first play of single authorship.

1894   July 12: Marries Pilar Moltó Campo-Redondo in Madrid.

1897   Begins his work of collaboration with Enrique García Álvarez.

1898   February 19: *El santo de la Isidra (Isidra's Saint)*. He had now produced thirty-nine plays.

1899   Made member Board of Directors of newly-formed *Sociedad de Autores Españoles* (Society of Spanish Authors).

1903   May 1: *El terrible Pérez (Terrible Pérez)*, the first of his *fresco* plays with García Álvarez.

1904   December 30: *Las estrellas (The Stars)*.

1907   December 17: *Alma de Dios (The Kindhearted Woman)*, his seventy-eighth production.

1912   His dispute and rupture with Enrique García Álvarez.

1916   April 14: *La Señorita de Trevélez (Miss Trevélez)*. Named as President of the *Círculo de Bellas Artes* (Fine Arts Club) of Madrid.

1918   March 9: Première of his first grotesque tragedy, *¡Que viene mi marido! (My Husband's Coming!)*.

1919   Ramón Pérez de Ayala publishes Volume Two of *Las máscaras (The Masks)*, containing two essays that help to consecrate Arniches' success.

1920   February 13: *Los caciques (The Bosses)*. He had now premièred 115 plays.

1921   October 19: *La heroica villa (The Heroic Town)*. December 12: Alicante pays tribute to Arniches as the city's Favorite Son.

1922   Appointed President of the Society of Spanish Authors.

1924   February 23: *Los milagros del jornal (Miracles from the Daily Wage)*.

1931   March 26: Madrid pays its tribute to Arniches.

1935   Receives the Madrid Medallion.

1936– He spends the years of the Spanish Civil War in Buenos Aires where,
1939   despite his unhappy and forlorn state, he continues to write for the
       theater.
1940   Returns with his wife to Spain.
1943   February 22: His daughter Rosario dies in Mexico.
       April 16: Arniches dies in Madrid at the age of 76. He had com-
       pleted his 191st play, *Don Verdades (Mr. Truth),* one day before
       his death.

CHAPTER 1

The Life and Times of Carlos Arniches

I *A Biographical Sketch*

CARLOS Jorge Germán Arniches y Barrera was the fifth of seven children and the only son of Carlos Arniches and María Antonia Barrera. Born October 11, 1866, Carlos spent his years of infancy and adolescence in Alicante, the provincial capital of his birth. The only evidence to suggest that Arniches might have been inclined toward the theater during these early years was his propensity to join classmates in staging short dramatic works while attending secondary school. Two of his fellow students were Rafael Altamira and Joaquín Dicenta. The first became a distinguished historian and literary critic; Dicenta, a defender of social justice in the modern realistic theater.

Alicante was far from being a serene and carefree Mediterranean city during Arniches' youth. Social unrest and violent political upheavals enveloped the scene. The citizenry responded to a long series of internal economic crises with a growing apprehension for the stability of their community. An epidemic of yellow fever had reduced the capital's population by five percent in 1870; three years later the Federalist insurrection of nearby Cartagena brought death and physical damage to Alicante. Subsequent Carlist incursions maintained a war-like atmosphere which, coupled with severe financial disturbances, "contributed to the exhaustion and prostration of the city, corroded by negligence, misery, and even hunger."[1]

The Arniches family suffered acutely from these social, political, and economic afflictions. Owing to local party manipulations, Carlos' father was relieved of his post as paymaster at the tobacco factory, only to be reinstated the following year, then rudely dismissed a second and final time. Carlos, reflecting in later years over this occurrence, writes that "poverty took possession of our home. All doors were closed to us, our horizons darkened, and we were obliged to abandon our beloved noble city."[2]

Arniches was not quite fourteen years of age when the family

departed from Alicante for Barcelona in 1880. The boy carried with
him a deep bitterness over the injustice of his father's dismissal. He
affirms that "an invincible hatred for politics was being forged,
silently and firmly, in his youthful heart."[3] This feeling was in-
delibly transferred to the stage many years later when he had
occasion to attack political corruption in *Los caciques (The Bosses)*,
one of his most forceful plays.

As his father's only son, Carlos sensed an obligation to sacrifice
his personal ambitions for the economic support of a large family
of girls. His five-year residence in Barcelona (1880–1885) produced
little by way of progress toward his ultimate career. Perhaps his
most significant activity of this period was news-reporting for
La Vanguardia, one of Barcelona's leading newspapers. While
the wage was only a pittance, Arniches relished this assignment
more than a concurrent menial but more lucrative employment as a
dry-goods clerk, for it placed him in contact with the literary climate
of the time.

Motivated by his suppressed ambitions to succeed in the world
of letters, Arniches moved to Madrid at the age of eighteen (1885).
For the first two years he lived under the protection of his aunt,
a stern and austere matron disposed to make a lawyer of Arniches
despite the young man's professed interest in literature. His defiance
of her dictates and her uncompromising severity resulted in a definitive rupture that found Arniches abandoned and penniless at the
age of twenty. He was now obliged to eke out a living without
recourse to family aid.

The years 1885 to 1887 were bleak for Arniches. He would later
reflect back on this period as the time of "a cruel and implacable
struggle" to survive, as that stage in his young life when strong
character was developed through adversity. The most positive
value of those years was the faith he gained "in the fortifying virtue
of work."[4] The labor he pursued was divided among the editorial
staffs of three insignificant newspapers.

Finally, in 1887, financial necessity compelled him to publish
his first work, a ninety-six page chronicle about the reign of Alfonso
XII entitled *Cartilla y cuaderno de lectura (Reading Primer)*.
Ramos observes that, in addition to having helped him resolve his
immediate economic hardships, the writing of this school primer
afforded Arniches his first authentic contact with the slum districts
of Madrid, owing to the research requirements for part of the text.[5]

Arniches would continue to extract inspiration from this source for the remainder of his long and distinguished career.

Within a year after the publication of his *Reading Primer,* Arniches staged his first play, *Casa Editorial (Publishing House),* a musical revue coauthored by his Alicante friend, Gonzalo Cantó. The work, teeming with contrived, fatuous jokes and bizarre puns, somehow managed to survive 150 performances. Following the première, Arniches was obliged to borrow a peseta from the dramatist Ventura de la Vega in order to phone his father and report the good news.[6] But by the end of the 150th staging, his financial problems at long last were behind him. The play brought him enough financial remuneration and commanded sufficient public and critical acclaim to persuade Arniches to devote the rest of his life to the theater.

He quickly wrote two more one-act musical revues, each a pattern of the preceding one, and both enjoyed greater success than *Publishing House.* However, with the resonant failure of yet another play of lyrical trivialities, staged in mid-November of 1888 with the title *Las manías (Manias),* Arniches decided to forsake these trifles of surface buffoonery in order to cultivate the sainete, a play form of one act that reflects the popular customs of the common people, and a type of drama which Arniches felt particularly well equipped to handle. His first sainete, *El fuego de San Telmo (St. Elmo's Fire),* was the initial work in a series of memorable early writings that secured for Carlos Arniches the undisputed recognition as Spain's "Illustrious *Sainetero.*"

The playwright's life after 1888 is a document of ascendant success, comfort, and prosperity. His name was respected and his presence honored throughout Spain. Late in his life this fame also accompanied him to Argentina. Following his death in 1943, his prestige has steadily increased owing to a continued staging of his best plays in many parts of the Hispanic world.

Save for an occasional visit to the Levantine coast, San Sebastián, or the Escorial—his preferred vacation spots—Arniches lived in urban Madrid for over fifty years. Here he was married at the age of twenty-seven (1894) to Pilar Moltó Campo-Redondo. Here too he raised his family of five children. And it was here that he was heralded as "a preeminent figure on the intellectual as well as the social order," having been named President of the *Círculo de Bellas Artes* (Fine Arts Club) in 1916.[7]

Not to be outdone by Alicante, where in December of 1921

he was confirmed that city's Favorite Son, Madrid's proud citizenry
bestowed a similar tribute upon him ten years later by declaring him
their Favorite Adopted Son and by changing the name of the
street commonly known as Calle Peñon to Calle Carlos Arniches.
He was one of five distinguished Spaniards to receive the coveted
Madrid Medallion in 1935, cited for having "raised the level of
Spanish theatrical literature to its high prestige."[8]

At the outbreak of the Spanish Civil War in 1936, Arniches
was spending the summer with his wife and two of his closest friends,
the dramatists Serafín and Joaquín Álvarez Quintero, at the
Escorial. He soon returned to Madrid, but fearing a wider spread
of the conflagration, he and his wife journeyed to Alicante, whence
they left in December of 1936 for Barcelona, embarking therefrom
for Marseilles, then on to Buenos Aires.

Arniches lamented his voluntary exile with a deep and brooding
anxiety. To have been separated from his homeland was vexing,
but to have left his many friends and loved ones in the midst of a
horrendous war was almost unbearable. He tried to forget his
anguish by busying himself as he had been wont to do for fifty years,
writing and staging plays. And the people of Buenos Aires responded
by according him an acclaim of unprecedented enthusiasm, but
still Arniches remained a bitter and lonesome man.

In short order the evidence of physical illness as an accompaniment to his mental grief was detected. His long-awaited return to
Spain following the war's conclusion in 1939 had to be delayed while
he recuperated from a second prostate operation. Finally, early in
1940, he and Pilar joyfully returned to their beloved country.

During the final three years of his life, Arniches wrote with his
accustomed vigor. "Men of genius," said William Hazlett," do
not excel in any profession because they labor in it, but they labor
in it, because they excel." This belief seemed to be Arniches' impulse
during his declining years, for despite ill health and chronic fatigue,
the playwright hearkened to the call of his public. His last play,
Don Verdades (Mr. Truth), was completed late Thursday afternoon,
April 15, 1943. The following day Arniches died of angina pectoris
and arteriosclerosis. The family attributed the rapidity of his decline
to the pain he had suffered upon learning of his daughter Rosario's
premature death in Mexico only two months earlier.

The burial of Carlos Arniches on Saturday, April 17, 1943,
occasioned one of the most extraordinary manifestations of public

mourning to have been recorded in Madrid's history. Perhaps only Lope de Vega's funeral before him and Alejandro Casona's since have rivaled the spectacle of an entire city's devotion to the memory of a beloved artist. A now-famous anecdote, related by Alfredo Marquerie, indicates the profound love of the Madrilenean people for the great Alicantine playwright: "When the burial of Arniches had been completed and the funeral procession was crossing the streets of the capital, a municipal policeman . . . asked someone walking in the retinue, 'Who was the deceased?' And when the policeman heard the *sainetero's* name, he removed his helmet, abandoned his post, and joined the procession with tears in his eyes. This brief but expressive popular anecdote effectively reveals the breadth of the wave of Arniches' work."[9]

II *The Man Arniches*

Arniches' life has every appearance of being a simple, unruffled, and somewhat prosaic existence. Having once attained recognition for his artistic talents, the man's popularity and prosperity became synonymous, and his habit patterns became so comfortably entrenched that one might have felt inclined to imagine that, as was the case with Immanuel Kant's regulated life, an invariable, geometric discipline had been prescribed to his every hour. Ramos speaks of the "rigorous chronometric existence" of his work schedule and daily habits.[10]

Arniches himself admitted a few months before his death that he had remained, since the age of fourteen, at the anvil of his labors with "an heroic perseverance. Every day, at nine, I am working. I première a play, I have a great success; the next day, at nine, back to work. I première a play, I am stunned by the scorn with which they greet me; the next day, at nine o'clock, back to work."[11]

A tall and slender man, Arniches displayed a comely black beard and a polished, slightly curved moustache during his youth. With his beard shaved off in later years and his small eyes bespectacled, his bearing was compared to that of "a Latin professor from a provincial school."[12] Throughout his life he was tailored meticulously and was never known to appear in public without his characteristic demeanor of social grace, refined manners, and consummate elegance.

He wrote his plays in his home on Montesquinza Street. His

studio was on the second floor. He always placed his favorite chair
to the right of the balcony overlooking the street. There, attired
in the most fashionable dressing gown with a white scarf around
his neck, using a portable desk at which he often wrote while
standing, he worked until one-thirty every afternoon. By two o'clock
he was eating with his family. Afterwards, following a brief rest,
he would journey to the theater to conduct the rehearsal of one of his
plays. "I rehearse for two hours," he once observed, "because my
strength goes no further. Rehearsals tire me, because I pour my
soul into them, and I even play out the parts when necessary. . . .
For this reason my works may turn out badly or tolerably, but
always well rehearsed."[13]

Before returning home for dinner at eight-thirty, followed by an
evening at the theater or at the movies with his wife, Arniches
frequently engaged in long walks by himself. Eschewing the serenity
and solitude of the Retiro Park, he favored at all times the bustle
and vivacity and fascination of old slums. These excursions into
Old Madrid provided him with relaxation, but, more importantly,
with inspiration for his writings. One need but read such sparkling
sainetes as *La fiesta de San Antón (St. Anthony's Festival)*, *El último
chulo (The Last Scamp)*, and *Los pícaros celos (Vile Suspicions)*
to appreciate the charm, the atmosphere, and the quaint characters
that Arniches encountered on his late afternoon walks.

Portillo gives the following account of these significant strolls:
"He employed his afternoons walking through the popular slums
of Madrid, studying, observing. He entered the taverns, the small
cafés, the pawnshops. He conversed with the strangest kind of
people and he had no qualms about going into the back alleys of
Madrid's *Injurias* District to learn about the lives of the derelicts
that he brought to the stage in such a luminous way."[14]

The image we have formulated of a calm and self-possessed
gentleman is suddenly shattered when we consider Arniches'
nervous state prior to and during the première of any one of his
nearly two hundred plays. His behavior was legendary even among
his co-workers. "Never have I known an author as timorous and
agitated as Don Carlos Arniches," reports one of his friends.[15]
"Arniches experienced a terrible panic in the presence of a debut,"
records another associate.[16] Miguel Mihura recalls having witnessed
Arniches' dreadful fear when the elderly playwright, despite having
written well over one hundred major works and being the most

acclaimed author of the time, would come down to the box office during a première and remain at young Mihura's side, "pallid, silent, unnerved, waiting for the public's verdict."[17]

One of Arniches' closest companions, Valeriano León, the actor whose very career was determined by playing the lead in ten of the author's best plays, remarked that Arniches' agony before the first performance of a play was so acute that he would disappear from the theater to roam the streets. León frequently had to lock him in his dressing room to prevent his escape. In the solitude of his prison, Arniches would often consume an entire *bote* of bicarbonate of soda before the end of the first act.[18] It is reported that on the night of the debut of *Yo quiero (I Want To)*, in January of 1936, Arniches depleted his supply of bicarbonate and then, under the nervous strain of the occasion, he unconsciously consumed a box of face powder, remarking afterwards in a nonchalant way that his bicarbonate had had a remarkable flavor, something akin to perfumed caramel.[19]

Arniches' nervousness at time resulted in irritability at play rehearsals. In some instances he would abandon the rehearsal then in progress, leaving the cast and his co-workers to complete their work without him. His occasional flare-ups nearly always subsided within a day's time with Arniches apologizing for his unjustified conduct. At one time, however, his petulance contributed to the irreparable breach with his most devoted collaborator, Enrique García Álvarez, about whom more will be said in a later chapter.

On some occasions Arniches' irritability would prompt him to vent his anger on his own manuscript. He would insist that the play be "touched up a bit" when the final rehearsals were not going as well as he desired. Portillo states that such affirmations filled the cast with terror, for they knew from experience that a minor "touch-up" meant the rewriting of an entire act. *La chica del gato (The Forlorn Girl)*, for example, a three-act comedy written to inaugurate the spring theater season of 1921, had its third act completely rewritten only twenty-four hours before the première.[20]

Happily for his wife and children, Arniches' emotional turbulence at the theater did not invade his home. He was a kind and loving father, devoted to the task of raising his youngsters on a high cultural plane. He provided them with frequent trips abroad, an active membership in social clubs, private studies in music, theater, and art, and professional training in the fields of their

choice. His three sons—Carlos, José María, and Fernando—
ultimately chose careers in architecture, law, and the military,
respectively. Now and then Arniches' generosity approached
indulgence; the family owned four automobiles at a time when the
possession of but one vehicle was considered a luxury.

Perhaps the cheerful liberality with which Arniches shared his
wealth stemmed from his vivid memories of his own boyhood
privations. Several of his plays show a dubious respect, and at
times an outright scorn, for money. Not infrequently his central
theme is man's lust for riches and the evils that correspond to an
unchecked materialism. To a large degree the playwright's spiritual
orientation and the positive preceptive force of his plays are the
product of an active religious faith which Arniches never questioned.
His writings attest to the fact that any adversity can be overcome or
compensated for by sacrifice, diligence, and an unwavering trust
in Christian virtues.

III *Arniches and the Generation of 1898*

Arniches' occasional position as social critic has led several
writers to link his name with the literary perspectives generated
by a number of his contemporaries.[21] The authors of the so-called
Generation of '98, grouped together somewhat tenuously by reason
of a common analytical concern for Spain's regeneration in the
wake of the Spanish-American War of that same year, enjoyed a
close historical proximity to Arniches by reason of their age, but
rarely came in close contact with the Alicantine playwright.[22]

Arniches' moral, sociological, and patriotic principles are in no
way antithetic to the attitudes of the Generation of '98. He partakes
of their serious concern for Spain's internal problems, a concern
we find vividly documented in some of his most important plays,
such as *La Señorita de Trevélez (Miss Trevélez), Los caciques
(The Bosses),* and *La heroica villa (The Heroic Town).* There is no
question as to his sincere and abiding interest in the regenerational
spirit that impelled some of Spain's greatest minds to denounce
national ills and to propose quick remedies, both practical and
idealistic. The impulse behind the conception of at least fifteen of
his major plays can be attributed to a deliberate and conscientious
resolve to awaken his spectators to the corrosion of sound values
in their midst and to encourage them anew with compassion and

optimism. In this sense, Arniches is, by conscience and sensitivity, a worthy member of that distinguished company of intellectuals usually assembled under the imprecise label of the Generation of '98.

In a larger sense, however, good reasons can be advanced for excluding Carlos Arniches from a literary grouping with such figures as Azorín, Pío Baroja, Jacinto Benavente, Antonio Machado, Miguel de Unamuno, and Ramón del Valle-Inclán. The very benevolence that underlies his devotion to Madrid and her people, his endeavor to immortalize the picturesqueness of present-day folk customs, his tolerance and compassion for human weakness, are by themselves factors that more or less distinguish his literary work from that of his peers.

An acrid hostility toward modern Madrid as reflected in the writings of Unamuno, Azorín, and Pío Baroja, is nowhere apparent in Arniches' plays.[23] Indeed, the same details about vulgar customs and popular urban types that irritate the aforenamed writers are exalted by Arniches in his short sainetes, farces, and full-length comedies. Azorín, for example, confines much of his exquisite descriptions to the small towns of Old Castile, dismissing Madrid for its "pain, ugliness, stridency, and death."[24] Arniches, on the other hand, equals the intensity and tenderness of Azorín's depictions with his own unique re-creation of the language and atmosphere of the Spanish capital.

Another aspect that sets Arniches apart from the Generation of '98 is the playwright's sustained cheerfulness. The disconsolate pessimism with which writers of the Generation of '98 condemn the present and view the future stands in sharp contrast with Arniches' optimistic tone. Arniches is unwilling to embrace the prevalent belief in a national misery. While his social and satirical criticism is undeniably incisive on occasion, one cannot speak of the presence of hopelessness, resignation, or embitterment in his works.[25] On the contrary, his theater, as Arturo Berenguer remarks, edifies with "kindness, clarity, and familiarity; it conveys the comfort of hope and the solution of faith in God and in the spirit."[26]

Alfredo Marqueríe points to still another difference between Arniches and the Generation of '98. He indicates the fact that of all the writers of that time, only Arniches and Benavente successfully appealed to a large majority of the public, and that of both these authors, Arniches alone, by virtue of his versatile command of language and his capacity for lifting current popular themes from the streets and homes and taverns of Madrid and reconstructing them on the stage, "drew himself near to all the public."[27] Elsewhere Marqueríe writes that "in its beginning the Generation of '98 appeared to depreciate the reader. It neither tried to elevate its public, nor descend or condescend to converse openly and frankly with it."[28]

Arniches, by contrast, professed to write only for the plain and simple people. While Benavente, Valle-Inclán, and Azorín pursued a purely literary goal, often looking beyond the Pyrenees to seek European currents of thought, Arniches limited his modest ambitions to the local milieu, from which he drew ideas and characters for his plays. Only after Ramón Pérez de Ayala, the renowned author and critic, brought Arniches' name into national prominence by writing several highly favorable essays on the literary value of his plays (1916–1919) did Arniches admit to the broadened universality of his artistry. He thereafter appeared to intensify the moral content of his plays without incurring any loss of popularity.

Is Arniches then a member of the famed generation? Considering the particulars cited above, weighed in the balance with the contributions and temperaments of his contemporaries, it must be said that Arniches has but a marginal relationship with respect to the innovations, the polemics, and the austere spiritual questionings that characterized the lives and writings of the authors of this group. Yet, with hearty patriotism, with good humor, Carlos Arniches raises many of the same issues, asks the same probing questions, and seeks the same elusive answers that perturbed his learned contemporaries. Perhaps he did as much, if not more, within the ambit of his widespread communication from the footlights with the Spanish people, transmitting a benign message of social and moral renovation, than did many of those who relied on weighty prose and lofty oratory with which to purge the nation. His was a robust concern for social order and human dignity, an attitude that brought a sense of poise and imperturbability to the inspired visions of a committed generation.

IV *Arniches and the Critics*

Shortly before his death, Arniches may have had a few of his inveterate detractors in mind when he appraised the reaction of the press and the critics to his work as being only "so-so."[29]

Then again, his apparent underestimation of his critical acclaim may have been but another indication of his characteristic modesty. There were ample reasons for Arniches to have been exultant in his final hours, for the response of important men in the world of letters weighed strongly in his favor.

Such was not the case when he began his career. Before the close of his first year of playwriting, Arniches had been branded with the pejorative epithet, "Carlos Currinche," a name coined from his last name to mean a tyro, an incompetent hack with grandiose pretensions to succeed. The word *currinche* was so frequently bandied about by the mudslingers of the Madrilenean press, that it was quickly admitted into official use by the Royal Spanish Academy to mean "among journalists, a beginner, a wretched writer."[30] The term lost its personal connotation soon after Arniches shifted from writing his trivial revues of 1888 to cultivate a traditional form of more literary substance: the sainete.

Negative criticism was minimal during the first decade of the twentieth century. This was the period of Arniches' most intense collaboration with other writers of the *género chico* and of his attachment for one-act musical plays. After 1910, however, he preferred two- and three-act plays, and his repertory disclosed a decisive departure from works of coauthorship. This alteration gave many critics a motive for comparing the *sainetero* of old with the new independent dramatist whose versatility was now apparent by the very nature of the tags he attached to his full-length plays: comedies, juguetes, sainetes, zarzuelas, farces, melodramas, pasatiempos, tragicomedies, and grotesque tragedies.

While in general Arniches fared well with his critics by varying his course and forging his own way, there were several members of the press who accused him of grafting timeworn properties, scenes, and character types from his conventional sainetes into the framework of his full-length dramas. This unfavorable and essentially unfounded criticism formed the basis for the position later assumed by José Vega and Nicolás González Ruiz in their respective charges that Arniches was a typical case of theatrical inertia, cleverly expanding the simple sainete to accommodate the playgoers of a new era.[31] The accusation was countered by José Bergamín, who maintains that Arniches never designed his plays after prescribed formulas.[32]

The turning point in Arniches' critical recognition began in 1916

with a series of articles by the aforementioned Pérez de Ayala.[33]
Ayala, a much admired novelist, poet, and literary critic, published
his most influential remarks about Arniches in 1919, in the second
of a two-volume collection of personal essays on contemporary
writers, entitled *Las máscaras (The Masks)*. Arniches had recently
staged two of his all-time best works, *Miss Trevélez* and *¡Qué
viene mi marido! (My Husband's Coming!)*. Ayala found in *Miss
Trevélez* a valid reason to endorse its author as a mature representative of the legitimate theater, a man whose former writings for the
género chico had now been surpassed in "truth, humanity, and
creative talent."[34] He lauded *My Husband's Coming!*, the first
of Arniches' grotesque tragedies, with unreserved gusto, enjoining
the world of higher criticism to give heed to the artistic virtues
of one of Spain's most remarkable playwrights.

Ayala's apology for Arniches is an impassioned exaggeration.
The unobjective bias by which he harshly condemns Jacinto Benavente in another essay from the same collection speaks for the
suspect nature of his critical posture. Nevertheless, the encomium
served to consecrate Arniches' name among the intelligentsia of his
time. Valle-Inclán now took notice of Arniches' theater, in fact
which also served to "lift his work from a sphere of popular anecdote
to a plane of national prominence."[35]

Although Arniches lamented the parallel that Ayala had drawn
between his theater and Benavente's,[36] he was thereafter indebted
to the author of *The Masks* and dedicated a volume of his sainetes
to him in 1918 saying, "You are my greatest success."[37]

Twenty years later Arniches reaffirmed his appreciation for
Ayala during an interview in Buenos Aires: "Even after having
begun to cultivate the *género chico*, I still was not considered a
literary power. But one day a critic as esteemed and as exacting as
Don Ramón Pérez de Ayala had the kind notion to devote to me an
extensive and laudatory analytical essay, demonstrating everything
that can be found in my theater containing a value of human observation and depiction of customs, . . . and since then, people began
to take me seriously."[38]

Few disparaging remarks were written about Arniches' theater
after 1920. His most zealous detractor appeared to be the drama
critic for *El Imparcial*, Enrique de Mesa, the only journalist of his
day to discredit the playwright's literary pretensions: "In the work
of Mr. Arniches there are no people of any kind, only stage puppets;

there is no human throb and vibration, only timeworn intrigues and deceits that extend from the front of the curtain to the back of the stage."[39]

Even the most hardened critics may temper their attacks. In Enrique de Mesa's case vituperation shifted to praise within ten years. Matilde Muñoz writes that he ended by affirming that the only theater of his day worthy of consideration and applause was the theater of Carlos Arniches.[40]

Other scholarly tributes served to enhance Arniches' reputation quite some time before he died. Azorín, for example, was one of his constant supporters. Writing occasionally for the Madrid newspaper *ABC,* Azorín defended Arniches from those critics who often passed lightly over the essence of his profound humor to remark about the surface comedy of the dialogue or situation. Arniches expressed his appreciation for the noted master's kind comments by dedicating the first edition of his last one-act sainete to him in 1924.[41]

Attempting to confirm the playwright's literary virtues without recourse to Ayala's exalting overstatements, Pedro Salinas wrote a convincing endorsement of Arniches in 1933. He concluded his study by saying that "Arniches . . . has now entered the rank of literary esteem which heretofore was conceded to only a few authors of learned and cultured background. He belongs, without an adjective to describe his background, in the front line of our contemporary dramatists."[42]

Federico García Lorca, one of Arniches' closest friends, who never failed to pay the older man a frequent visit with a gift of his favorite candy, gave an enthusiastic expression to his feelings about the poetic atmosphere of the *sainetero*'s writings: "Don Carlos Arniches is more of a poet than almost all those who are writing theater in verse nowadays. There can be no theater without a poetic atmosphere, without invention . . . There is fantasy in the most humble sainete of Don Carlos Arniches . . . The work of enduring success is that which has been written by a poet, and there are a thousand works built on well-written verse that are shrouded in their graves."[43]

Mention has been made of Berenguer Carísimo's criticism. He was the first critic to honor Arniches with a book. His monograph, entitled *El teatro de Carlos Arniches (The Theater of Carlos Arniches),* was presented personally to the exiled playwright on the occasion of his induction into the Ateneo Iberoamericano, one of the highest honorary tributes to be awarded a living artist in the Argentine Republic. Berenguer's book, considering its proximity in time to the playwright's life, is an excellent general analysis of his theater.

Following the playwright's death, higher criticism of Arniches' role in the development of the Spanish farce has continued to bestow favor on his name. Writers of recognized stature, such as Dr. Gregorio Marañón, Alfredo Marqueríe, José Monleón, and others whose names are mentioned in the course of this study, have contributed essays that will help to assure Arniches a permanent place among the most admired authors of modern Spanish literature.

CHAPTER 2

Arniches and the Spanish Farce

A RNICHES' devotion of over half a century to the depiction of Madrilenean life and customs is most clearly documented in his writings for the *género chico,* one-act dramas with or without music. So completely did his language and style take root in the popular theater of his day that, by the time he had staged his first three-act play at the age of thirty-three, he had already been proclaimed the master of that abbreviated form of comedy which had wooed an entire generation of theatergoers.

Too often, however, critics have been disposed to type Arniches as a singular product of a determined age. They have viewed his penchant for characterizing colorful local figures, such as Madrid's low-class ruffian (the *chulo*), his fondness for describing the slum districts of Madrid, and his tendency to re-create the vernacular of the rank and file of Madrid's low-born masses, as justifiable criteria for classifying him as a regionalistic genre writer.

The ultimate value of his work must lie elsewhere if Arniches is to take his place among the great dramatists of the Spanish theater. Were his literary merit confined within the narrow limits of a particular era or reduced to the strict relationship of an affinity for his adopted city, then time would surely relegate his name to oblivion and transform his creative writings into documents of mere historical interest.

While a great man's distinction is earned in the workshop of his generation, much of his genius resides in the clever use he makes of his legacy from the past. That which causes the name of Carlos Arniches to loom large among the multitude of now-forgotten writers of the *género chico* is the fact that he knew how to correlate his natural talent with an understanding of the long and glorious tradition of Spanish folk theater, and did so better than any playwright of his time. His theater is more than a testimony of exquisite craftsmanship; in the one act comediettas, zarzuelas, sainetes, revues, pasillos, entremeses, and comic sketches that he wrote, presenting with veracity the cares and the struggles of the common people in a given locality, Arniches reveals his indebtedness to the little farcical masterpieces in prose or verse that constitute a large part of the literary heritage he received from many illustrious predecessors.

It is in this broader perspective that the playwright's contributions to the *género chico* should be appraised. In their totality, his shorter writings warrant an evaluation not alone as chronicles of the lower class of Madrilenean society and of that city's vernacular, but more important, as a vital segment of Spanish dramatic history. Transcending mere localism and dialectal entrenchment, they serve to link the *costumbrismo* (the portrayal of everyday life and customs) and the humor of the *género chico* with the stock themes and characters of former generations. Indeed, until another school appears to improve upon Arniches' work in the popular theater, his one-act plays will continue to represent the consummation of a rich tradition of realistic theater pieces. They reinforce the revival of a nationally popular theater that came of age in the last decade of the nineteenth century.

It is our present aim, therefore, to outline the evolution of the one-act farce in Spanish literature, observing its major trends and important literary representatives, in order to relate this development to the artistic labors of Carlos Arniches, its foremost proponent in modern times.

I *The Entremés*

The entremés, as defined by early annotators of dramatic literature, was "a brief, jocose, and burlesque performance, usually inserted between the acts of a play to provide greater variety or to entertain and amuse the audience."[1] Later explanations of the term have only elaborated upon this basic definition, reciting the immutability of the entremés's farcical nature and reaffirming the fact that its original structural purpose was that of providing comic relief as an attendant interlude for the exalted flights of dramatic expression in the love and honor plays of the Renaissance and Golden Age.

Edwin Honig echoes this traditional description with reference to the eight famous Cervantine entremeses: "The interlude [entremés] is usually dominated by its farcical tone. It is made up of a short incident and is meant to be performed between the acts of a full-length play in order to quiet an audience. It deals with stock characters and a temporarily unhinged situation reassembled at the end by a token banquet, dance, or marriage. In these respects little had changed since the days of ancient Plautine comedy, on which were patterned the situations and character types of the entremés."[2]

That the entremés functioned "to quiet an audience" was but part of its role. Not infrequently the exuberant spontaneity of a plebeian farce also provoked loud outbursts of hilarity, inducing a large contingent of the spectators to anticipate the parenthetical parody or satire of each entremés with more delight than the denouement of the principal play.[3] More often than not, a good pair of entremeses confirmed the success of a mediocre play, as one writer of the past century observed: "By inserting two entremeses of merit, the author of a poor play would give it crutches to keep it from falling, while for the author of a good play, the entremeses gave it wings to help it soar."[4]

The popular success of the entremés was inevitable. Its source material was found among the people, in their waggish tales, anecdotes, and picaresque yarns. Its stock themes and formulas were derived from that inexhaustible storehouse of literary gleanings: the common folklore of Western tradition.

Recent criticism reiterates the conventional view that the original entremés had its origin in the atmosphere of the riotous medieval carnival, in which the physical instincts, eating, and drinking were glorified.[5] Some elements of universal currency in the farce, such as its characteristic whipping scene, are traceable to the Italian *commedia dell'arte,* while the imaginative re-creation of everyday language and the emphasis on base conduct are allegedly products of the brazen secular plays of Spain's own medieval past, the so-called derision plays *(juegos de escarnio)* and the related playlets dealing with student pranks *(juegos escolares),* none of which is extant, though the genre is alluded to in early chronicles that condemned their licentious and irreverent properties.

Owing to its heterogeneous roots, the entremés has been labeled a genre of enormous fluctuation, depending for its material on other literary and nonliterary forms. Eugenio Asensio speaks of the entremés as "an unstable genre, perpetually seeking its form, zigzagging between comic tales and revues, fantasy and writings of everyday life. It relies on all assimilable forms of amusement, such as dance, music, mummery. This fluctuation, this constant mobility, is in part conditioned by its nature as a secondary and dependent genre."[6]

II Infancy of the Entremès: Before Cervantes

Because few medieval plays have been preserved, the history of the Spanish farce is often said to begin in the late fifteenth century with Juan del Encina (1469?–1529?). Encina's sixty-eight musical compositions and two playful amorous eclogues (Eglogas amorosas) are said to be forerunners of the modern zarzuela.[7] His coarse Auto del repelòn (The Hair-Pulling Skit) involves the kind of vulgar slapstick that has often accompanied the rise and the later revivals of popular interlude writings. Encina's "profane" plays introduce shepherds who evoke laughter through a sportive imitation of upper-class manners and courtly love.

A contemporary of Encina, Garcí Sánchez de Badajoz (1460?–1526?), is considered by one critic to be the intermediary between early religious drama and the later farce in Spain.[8] Badajoz inserted comic episodes in his religious allegories, much in the same way that Encina included scenes of low comedy with the aristocratic tone of his eclogues. His importance to the farce lies in his having introduced many of the stock types of the period, such as the boastful soldier and the canting sacristan. His occasional satire on the clergy and on public officials, citing their dishonesty and injustice, reinforces one writer's contention that "social satire is to play a considerable part in the entremés as it develops."[9]

Continuing the pattern set by Encina and Badajoz, a third writer of occasional farce is Lucas Fernández (1474?–1542), who is credited with having turned the conventional pastoral play into comic disputes between schematically drawn shepherds. One of his major accomplishments as continuator of commonplace themes was to give considerable importance to the figure of the boastful soldier, a type established in the miles gloriosus of Plautine comedy.[10]

Gil Vicente (1465–1536?) likewise added a small handful of lively costumbrista pieces to the history of the farce in its formative stage. His ironic view of certain familiar types, from the young enamored swain to the licentious old man, is presented with a vivacity and wit unequalled in his day.

The playwright to whom literary historians generally attribute

the role of having provided the greatest impetus to the early development of humor in the Spanish drama is Bartolomé Torres Naharro
(1476?–1531?). His innovations include the introduction to the
Spanish stage of the witless low comedian (the *gracioso*), a type and
label perpetuated in the comic of Golden Age comedies, the buffoon
of the zarzuela, and the simpleton of many *género chico* writings,
including Arniches' mischievous *fresco* and roguish *chulo,* in which
are combined the arrogance of the classical braggart *(el fanfarrón)*
and the exasperating indiscretion of the *bobo* (simpleton).

Torres Naharro also contributed the first important models
for the comedy of intrigue. His works have been noted for their
anticlerical satire, well-developed characterizations, and the use
of different languages within the context of single plays. In his
Comedia soldadesca, for example, recruits from various countries
and regions speak in their respective dialects. Parody and satire
are thereby intended, a device not unlike that employed by Arniches
in several of his early sainetes.

Often called the creator of the entremés, Lope de Rueda (1510?–
1565) continued the popular tradition of the early farce by writing
ten short plays of actualized folklore, known as sketches *(pasos),*
owing to their rapid action and simple plots. Despite their brevity
and superficiality, Rueda's pasos were of such excellent literary
quality as to warrant high praise from Cervantes in his celebrated
prologue to his collection of *Eight Plays and Eight Interludes:
New and Never Performed* (1615).[11]

It should be noted that the paso is but another word for entremés.
The two terms were used interchangeably by Juan de Timoneda
(1490?–1583), the versatile exploiter and bookseller whose commercial appropriations of Lope de Rueda's writings, following
his old friend's death, accounted in large measure for the propaga-
tion of Rueda's fame. That the paso by name preceded the entremés
and gave rise to the latter is a conceded fact of literary history, but
that it differed in any significant way, either in its purpose or structure, is a matter of such minor importance that critics have rarely
been troubled by anything beyond a mere semantic distinction.

The farces of Lope de Rueda's day bring together the stock devices
and themes that were to constitute the common repository from
which successful playwrights would draw material for many
generations. Such topics as disguises, mistaken identities, funny
names, threats, beatings, insatiable hunger, a craving for alcohol,

name-calling, feigned madness, and dreams—none of which is foreign to the *género chico*—gained great impetus in the hands of Lope de Rueda, whose own sources of inspiration included the Italian and Latin comedies, the Spanish picaresque genre, *La Celestina,* and the contemporary theater of his time. Also embodied in his pasos we find a sizable assortment of picturesque lower-class types. These figures are realistically portrayed and are harmonized to the unfolding of the action and to the author's creditable use of prose for colloquial expression.[12] With respect to language, Rueda's dialogue is a model of vernacular discourse without losing its literary quality. As Carlos Arniches endeavored to do with the *chulo* dialect of Madrid over three hundred years later, Lope de Rueda bent the flow of language to the inflections of daily conversation, exploiting a variety of jargons and dialects in "a nation politically united but linguistically diversified."[13]

Lope de Rueda's salient contribution to the theater is his perfection of the twin farcical character types that Eugenio Asensio has termed the two poles of the *entremés.* The first is that colorful incarnation of ignorance and foolishness, the simple fool or *bobo,* whose social maladjustment makes him the object of taunting and jest. The second is that swell-headed ruffian whose feigned eloquence and exorbitant airs and boastfulness label him a social misfit wherever decorum is observed: the cowardly braggart or *fanfarrón.*

The constant reappearance of these figures in dramatic literature is as time-honored as a proverb. The negative qualities they embody provide a contrast to the virtues of the hero, parody to the actions of the protagonist, tension to the conflict, and surface ridicule to the characters themselves. Incapable of perceiving logic and latitude in the chain of human actions, the *bobo*'s narrow vision of reality leads inevitably to disaster. Similarly unprosperous is the fortune of the unheroic bully, whose mental deficiency is an overweening pride in his physical prowess and seductive charms.

One often thinks of Lope de Rueda's laughable characters, extracted from low-class society, when reading the early writings of Carlos Arniches. In the same way that Lope de Rueda centers the action of his pasos around the foolish conduct of the simpleton or the arrogance of the boaster, Arniches fashions several of his one-act farces around the arresting figure of the Madrilenean *fresco,* an amalgam of Lope de Rueda's archetypal fool and the swaggerer. The *fresco* possesses the *bobo*'s characteristic laziness, incontinence, and absurd logic, together with the *fanfarrón*'s physiological obsession with love and drink and his reckless conceit.

In Chapter Three we will describe the comic figure of the *fresco* within the context of five specific plays in which he appears. For the time being it will serve our purpose to observe that the *fresco* is a direct descendent of the Renaissance *bobo-fanfarrón* and the Golden Age *gracioso-rufián* combinations, and that it gave rise in turn to the more complicated rogues to be found in Arniches' two- and three-act sainetes and in the grotesque tragedies.

In the fifty years that intervene between the death of Lope de Rueda (1565) and the appearance of Cervantes' eight interludes (1615), the entremés gradually seeks its independence as a respected genre. It still continues to receive nourishment for its subject matter and tone in the full-length Spanish *comedia,* taking sustenance from other literary zones as well, in a manner typical of its original parasitical nature. However, the simplicity of the comic episode now begins to give way to involved parody, either as a contrast to or a prolongation of the major *comedia,* with a corresponding heightening of literary attention to action and dialogue. Caricature and burlesque become more prevalent, responding to a popular fancy for the satire of social, moral, and intellectual extravagances. This trend is particularly apparent in the anonymous farces of the period and results in a mechanized typing of characters. More urban figures, most of them ridiculous individuals lifted from a miscellany of professions and stations of Madrilenean life, complete with their peculiar street vocabulary, make an entrance onto the Spanish stage. These become the prototypes of humor from which Cervantes, Quiñones de Benavente, Ramón de la Cruz, Ricardo de la Vega, and Carlos Arniches will develop personalities of engaging complexity and expanded human dimension.

Another phenomenon that emerges during these years is the rise in popularity of octosyllabic and hendecasyllabic verse to accompany the more conventional use of prose in the entremés. The shorter form of versification, with assonance in alternating lines (the *romance*), is generally reserved for passages rendered in song, while the longer meter remains close to common speech. With the adoption of verse—which is a predominant characteristic by the year 1620—the reality depicted by the entremés becomes highly stylized, and the possibilities for comic inventiveness and originality increase. This expanded freedom to materialize fantasy and language within the atmosphere

of dance and song is the most significant step leading to the interlude's eventual emancipation from the *comedia*. Quiñones de
Benavente's hybrid compositions—entremeses performed entirely
in song or dance—are the logical outgrowth of this trend toward
versified musical entertainment. The end result of his labors will be
the formulation of the Spanish zarzuela.

III *Ascendancy of the Entremés: Cervantes*

With Miguel de Cervantes Saavedra (1547–1616), the entremés
is accorded the master's seal. His six entremeses in prose and two in
verse have been acclaimed "the most beguiling things Cervantes ever
wrote."[14] Stressing the author's virtuosity in the technical aspect of
characterization, Edwin Honig praises "the extraordinary freedom
of the characters to be themselves in a framework of considerable
but not unlimited fluidity."[15] Others have extolled the "marvelous,
fresh, and living dialogue of the artist," citing his incomparable
superiority over "the ancient writers of farce."[16] Still other critics
celebrate the playwright's skill in fusing a world of dynamic reality
with a subtle and alluring dimension of poetic fantasy: "In the
discovery of the interrelationship between those worlds and in
having known how to give artistic plasticity to that discovery, lies
Cervantes' great genius."[17]

The fact that multiple levels of meaning can be ascribed to the
Cervantine interludes attests to the crowning success of the genre
in the early years of the seventeenth century. Under Cervantes the
entremés changes in perspective, shedding its reputation as a
raucous offshoot of the estimable *comedia,* to gain wider respect,
even among discriminating playgoers, as a legitimate prescription
for evoking laughter, intermingled with a realistic portrayal of
customs, language, and people.

While making use of the stock comic types, Cervantes expands and
humanizes his characters, imbuing them with self-expression, mature
reflection, and a diversification of attitudes to widen their choices
from among several alternatives. In short, Cervantes treats his
creations with psychological depth. His multidimensional types
include representatives from "the contemporary underworld and the
middle- and lower-brow society of small towns and cities—country
bumpkins, divorce courts, magicians, imposters, unemployed
soldiers, unsheltered students, ineffectual husbands, saucy maids,
irritable housewives, fatuous sacristans, garrulous whores."[18]

In one of his best-known farces, *La cueva de Salamanca (The Cave of Salamanca)*, he introduces the conventional figure of the cuckold, in this case a credulous old man who is cleverly fooled by his young wife and a starving student. Public and church officials are lampooned in *La elección de los alcaldes de Daganzo (Choosing a Councilman in Daganzo)*, wherein Cervantes satirizes the church's interference in civil issues. He portrays with burlesque humor the problems stemming from incompatible marriages, especially those in which there is a wide age difference between husband and wife, in *El juez de los divorcios (The Divorce Court Judge)* and *El viejo celoso (The Jealous Old Husband)*. In *La guarda cuidadosa (The Hawk-eyed Sentinel)* a braggart soldier loses his scullery maid to a smug sacristan. The hypocrisy and folly of an entire town are satirized in one of the most celebrated interludes of all time, *El retablo de las maravillas (The Wonder Show)*.

In each and all of these comic treatments, Cervantes amplifies the human element, lessens histrionic gestures, complicates the actions, and takes an ironic and sympathetic view toward the creatures of his imagination. His is an example of considerable merit for successive generations to follow.

IV *Supremacy of the Entremés: Quiñones de Benavente*

Luis Quiñones de Benavente (1598?–1651) gave the entremés its definitive form.[19] Considered "a genius for comic situation and dialogue," he became one of the most revered and imitated writers of the seventeenth century.[20] According to Luis Astrana Marín, between 1620 and 1650 one or another of Quiñones' interludes was staged at every theatrical festival in Spain.[21] His writings represent the most authentic criticism of the Spanish society of his day. They also embrace all of the diversified characters of the genre in its period of plenitude.

It would be a difficult task to provide a useful thematic classification of Quiñones de Benavente's works. His extraordinary versatility in having produced nearly nine hundred pieces of music, verse, and prose is by itself an accomplishment not easily summarized.[22] Those who have studied his theater attest to the fact that he dealt with just about every type of situation, and that his success as the so-called "Monarch of the Entremés" was ascribable to his masterful control over the exercise of poetry, song, and choreography, the

vehicles by which he depicted social customs, caricatured contemporary fashions and ideas, moralized with elegance, and, above
all, entertained his public with a brilliant stylized comedy that ran
the gamut from sophisticated satire to outlandish harlequin buffoonery. Eugenio Asensio has affirmed that Quiñones' "histrionic
mastery, his virtuosity with dialogue, his prodigious facility for
constructing with so little a comic entertainment, assure him the
primacy of the genre."[23]

Quiñones was one of the few playwrights of light comedy who
appealed to all levels of spectators. His verbal fluidity and discerning
insight into people commanded a large following that lasted for
several decades after his death. This popularity contributed to the
high regard accorded the entremés in the seventeenth century as a
genre of large social value. Under Quiñones the entremés became
the most immediate form of realistic expression of Spanish life,
albeit bizarre and carnivalesque on occasion, to have appeared since
the rise of the picaresque novel and before the incomparable
etchings of Francisco de Goya.

The enormous vitality of Quiñones de Benavente's realistic theater
established a precedent for future *entremesistas,* including Carlos
Arniches, to follow. His farces successfully integrated characterization, humor, and dialogue with the social scene, thus synthesizing in
a given literary form an artistic documentation of regional flavor and
historical value. Quiñones was for the era of the classical entremés
what Arniches represents to the modern theater of the *género chico,*
namely: an eminent entertainer whose fluent expression reaches
into all social levels to expound on the virtues, vices, and customs
of the common people.

V *The Zarzuela*

Similar to the Italian operetta, the Spanish zarzuela is a musical-
dramatic work of abbreviated length in which a slight plot is
developed through the medium of spoken dialogue, either in prose or
verse. The dialogue alternates with sung or orchestrated passages.
The long and quite involved history of the zarzuela, perhaps of more
interest to musicologists than to students of literature, is treated in
other available studies and requires no detailed repetition here.[24]
It should suffice to point out that the introduction of music, dance,
and song as an accompaniment to, or as an intercalation between,

the spoken lines of a play dates back to the beginning of dramatic literature. In Spain this corresponds to such extant forms as Encina's eclogues, Lope de Rueda's pasos, and the entremeses of Timoneda, which were occasionally preceded and often followed by spirited musical compositions sung by members of the cast.

By the seventeenth century the public's attachment for musical interludes had induced many Spanish playwrights to collaborate with noted musicians in the production of complete dramatic spectacles featuring brilliant musical scores, exotic costumes, and dazzling stage effects.[25]

The staging of these musical *comedias* was a national pastime before the term "zarzuela" was ever adopted. The name first appeared in reference to the royal family's patronage of lyrical dramas at La Zarzuela, a palace residence at El Pardo near Madrid. The word "zarzuela" is derived from *zarza,* meaning bramble bush, alluding to the thorny bushes that surrounded the palace of that name.

In view of the Crown's support for the zarzuela and the subsequent importation of Italian musicians, composers, and musical forms during the eighteenth century, public taste shifted abruptly from a cultivation of national traditions to an assimilation of foreign products. In general, the theater became an exclusive form of diversion for the elite, and the zarzuela itself became longer, more complicated, ornate, and operatic.

A single exception to this eighteenth-century Italianate phenomenon was the zarzuela writing of Ramón de la Cruz, whose musical compositions after 1768 consisted wholly of popular Spanish airs and depicted popular Spanish customs in a realistic manner.

It was not until the mid-nineteenth century that theatergoers grew weary of overlyricized performances. Once again the shorter version of musical entertainment was adopted, in which singing and dancing were subordinate to stage action. This was the era of the widely acclaimed *género chico.*

The zarzuela was taken up by over one hundred writers during the forty years that the *género chico* reigned supreme (1870–1910). While often omitted from the roster of distinguished zarzuela authors, in deference to his superior accomplishments as a writer of sainetes, Carlos Arniches contributed in a significant measure to the dissemination and popularity of the zarzuela at the turn of the century. As was the case with Ramón de la Cruz a century earlier, whose first play was a zarzuela and who later interwove musical pieces of varying length among his sparkling sainetes, Arniches likewise initiated his dramatic career with a multitude of zarzuela-like productions, then continued favoring many kinds of musical compositions over the nonmusical comedy throughout the first twenty-five years of his writing for the stage.

In specific terms, if we adhere strictly to Arniches' own designations, we must credit him with having written the text for thirty-two zarzuelas. Twice that number would be more precise, however, for the playwright's labels are markedly arbitrary. Quite often his lyrical pieces are rendered under names other than zarzuela with no appreciable difference in content from that of the conventional operatic form.[26]

In 1915, for example, his amusing morality play about bullfighting and envy, *El chico de Las Peñuelas (The Boy of Las Peñuelas)*, was staged as a lyrical sainete, but structurally it was no different from any zarzuela of similar length, such as *La estrella de Olimpia (The Star of Olympia)*, a play about a loose girl's change of heart in a wartime setting, premièred later that same year. The only apparent distinction between Arniches' zarzuelas and his other musical writings is the presence in most of the former of a larger cast and of more orchestration.

Arniches cultivated three types of zarzuelas: the simple, one-act variety, the melodrama, and the zarzuela of entanglement. Those of the first grouping lay stress upon lighthearted pranks and raillery in a semi-bizarre atmosphere, as illustrated by the trilogy of lyricized ghost tales that Arniches wrote in collaboration with Gonzalo Cantó and Celso Lucio between 1890 and 1892: *La leyenda del monje (The Legend of the Monk)*, *Los aparecidos (The Ghosts)*, and *Las campanadas (The Stroking of the Bell)*. Each of these comic zarzuelas manifests a spirit of playful banter prevailing over a simple plot. The briskness of the action is upheld by the restlessness, fervor, and spirited music of the townsfolk, whose superstitions and wild imaginations add a mixed tone of humor and suspense to the alleged supernatural events transpiring around them.

The second kind of zarzuela, the musical melodrama, includes such titles as *Doloretes, El puñao de rosas (A Handful of Roses), Los granujas (The Urchins)*, and *Los chicos de la escuela (The School-boys)*, all of which enjoyed great commercial success, appealing overall to audiences enthralled by gay and sentimental plots in which noble virtues are lauded and evil is condemned. The zarzuela of entanglement, on the other hand, is a musical drama that highlights the complications of stage action and character dilemmas over an exhibition of popular melodies. Musical segments are perceptibly reduced. A moderate shift takes place away from vocal and instrumental entertainment towards an emphasis on warm, human situations. These writings correspond to Arniches' prolific years of co-authorship with Enrique García Álvarez. They include some eight playlets staged from 1905 to 1912. The plays themselves are of relative merit, but the period in which they were composed is of great importance: it represents the most significant maturing phase of Arniches' early career, the time during which his versatile handling of theater forms surpasses mere conformity with a traditional pattern. Of this period, when Arniches ventures into the realm of a personal style and original technique, more will be stated in our section corresponding to his collaboration with García Álvarez.

VI *The Sainete*

The sainete is the most recent form of light comedy to have evolved from the time-honored entremés. Its compact framework, its cargo of humor and realism, and its function to amuse the spectator are the sainete's most obvious connections with antiquity.

The word "sainete," originally applied to a small morsel of fat, marrow, or brains awarded by the hunter to his deserving falcon,[27] was adopted in the mid-seventeenth century to mean, in a figurative sense, a delectable tidbit of theater entertainment, abounding in savory good humor.[28] "As a theatrical term," states C. E. Kany, "it was used almost indiscriminately to denote any short play, as entremés, baile, loa, etc. Later, however, the use of the word was restricted."[29]

About midway into the eighteenth century it was customary to designate the interlude performed between the first and second acts of a longer comedy as an entremés, while the same type of entr'acte placed between the second and third acts was called a sainete.[30]

Despite their juxtaposition as companion pieces wedged between the acts of full-length plays, there is, as G. T. Northup observes, a structural distinction between the entremés and the sainete: "The sainete is a comic, one-act theatrical piece, longer than the entremés, introducing more characters, and with a somewhat more ambitious plot, portraying realistically various social types, and satirizing human vices and foibles."[31]

In its development during the eighteenth century, the sainete acquired a fixed meaning and became the most specialized form of popular comedy, providing an accurate reflection of the life and thought of the common people. According to Kany, "it was now a play of one act, in verse, with but little plot, . . . the comic element dominating in the dialogue. The characters were usually chosen from the lower classes of society, whose language and manners were closely imitated. . . . The time of the performance was not to exceed twenty-five minutes."[32]

The sainete's expansion in the late eighteenth century parallels the entremés' degeneration. The entremés fell into such a stage of decay and obscenity that it was finally suppressed in 1780. At first Spanish audiences welcomed the charm and freshness of the sainete as an antidote counteracting the tasteless effects of the entremés' crude jokes and burlesques. Then, as the popular theater of Ramón de la Cruz caught on, with all of its refined literary expression of Madrid customs, the public accepted it on its own merits, praising its intent to glorify national types, manners, and expressions. The revival of the polished farce was short-lived, however, for the more than four hundred sainetes written by Ramón de la Cruz virtually disappeared from the Spanish theater upon the death of this playwright in 1794. The sainete did not reappear with vigor for another seventy-five years.

Satirical humor and caricature prevailed in the sainetes of the late nineteenth century. The major *saineteros* exploited conventionally popular themes. Their light and superficial treatments conveyed above all a tone of sentimentality, tenderness, and wit, but with a depiction of Spanish customs that was faithful to life.

Despite its mechanized form, the short farce commanded sufficient public regard to be compared for its realistic impact on society as a part of the same school that produced the highly successful theater of pure or serious drama, *la alta comedia* (high comedy). The Spanish high comedy began earlier with Leandro Fernández de Moratín (1760–1828), continued through Ventura de la Vega (1807–1865), Adelardo López de Ayala (1828–1879), and Manuel Tamayo y Baus (1829–1898), to reach its pinnacle with the great twentieth-century playwright, Jacinto Benavente (1866–1954), and his followers.

High comedy is a term used to distinguish serious drama from farce. It "rests upon an appeal to the intellect and arouses 'thoughtful' laughter by exhibiting the inconsistencies and incongruities of human nature and by displaying the follies of social manners. The purpose is not consciously didactic or ethical, though serious purpose is often implicit in the satire which is not infrequently present in high comedy."[33] It might further be stated that high comedy seeks "the approval of a smaller, more discriminating, albeit less lucrative audience, scorning devices of mere popular appeal."[34]

This distinction between high and low comedy has not always cast the sainete in favorable light with the critics. Since the time of the sainete's initial triumph under Ramón de la Cruz in the eighteenth century, to the period of its superlative development by Ricardo de la Vega, Carlos Arniches, and the Quintero brothers in the twentieth century, the form has been hastily and unjustifiably dismissed as a shallow and frivolous satellite of the legitimate stage, unworthy of comparison with full-length plays. The true value of the sainete is best appreciated, however, by noting the specific contributions to the genre by its best representatives over the past 250 years. Their works will continue to be read and staged as long as the charm of popular customs, types, and language endures.

VII *Ramón de la Cruz and Arniches*

The sainete was brought to full development by Ramón de la Cruz (1731–1794), who preserved the purity of the language of the lower classes and immortalized numerous unforgettable types from that stratum of Madrilenean society.[35] His little plays, as Kany writes, "are of incalculable historic value, not only for his portraits of types and customs, but also for his humorous references to insignificant events of the day, for which we should look in vain elsewhere . . . He took the sainete from the low level to which it had sunk by the middle of the eighteenth century and raised it to the height and dignity of a comedy of manners by substituting vital characters for the usual conventional types. The humor of his sainetes is of a sort more refined and infinitely more subtle than the broad and boisterous horseplay of his predecessors and contemporaries. His light but accurate touch, his scintillating and realistic dialogue are qualities which even his worst enemies admitted he possessed in an unusually high degree. He put into the mouths of his characters, and thus preserved to posterity, hundreds of popular words and phrases which have long since fallen into desuetude and for which only fruitless search could be made elsewhere. Students of the language are greatly indebted to him."[36]

Ramón de la Cruz's major legacy to Arniches is his propensity for setting his sainetes in the street or in a tenement courtyard and dramatizing the bustle and animation of crowds. Arniches also inherits his predecessor's practice of lifting characters out of real life. Cruz affirmed that he wrote only that which the truth dictated to him, that his sainetes were copies of that which his eyes had seen and his ears had heard, and represent therefore an authentic document of his century.[37] In like manner Arniches proclaims that absolutely all of his characters are faithful copies of reality.[38] A third similarity is noted in the use by both authors of dialect and slang. Their characters often use bad grammar and exchange repartee in a vernacular characteristic of the inhabitants of the old, poor districts of Madrid.

The chief difference between the two *saineteros* lies in, first, their respective attitudes toward the common people, and second, the structuring of their plays. With regard to the first difference, Cruz delights in accentuating the mistakes of the lower classes, ridiculing at times their ignorance and gullibility. While he reserves his sharpest criticism for upper-class manners and middle-class behavior, Cruz's attitude toward the proletariat is generally one "of sympathy tinctured with mild amusement," although in nearly all of his sainetes he pokes fun at his characters.[39] Arniches, on the other hand, idealizes his creations, placing emphasis upon their noble points. He allows the foibles of his heroes to give meaning to moral issues rather than evoke laughter for their own sake. Alfonso Paso carries this point one step further by stating that for the first time in the sainete, Arniches brings "compassion for the poor little people, elevating the humble to fantastic heights." Arniches thus establishes "the highest level of communication between the people and an author to have been attained in two centuries.[40]

Concerning the construction of their plays, Cruz tends to avoid a central, unifying action and is more intent on sketching the color and gaiety of popular customs. Arniches goes a step beyond the mere depiction of *costumbrismo* by enlarging the canvas with a clear conception of the human drama behind the folkloric scene. Perhaps these differences can best be appreciated by reading Cruz's sainete, *La pradera de San Isidro (The Meadow of San Isidro)*, 1766, in comparison with Arniches' play on the same festive theme, *Isidra's Saint* (1898).

VIII   *Ricardo de la Vega and Arniches*

Considered the best of the nineteenth-century *saineteros* before Arniches, Ricardo de la Vega (1839–1910) wrote clever farces with little plot but much realistic portrayal of life in Madrid, particularly of the lower classes. Among his best known works are *Pepa la frescachona (The Very Robust Pepa)* and *La verbena de La Paloma (The Night Festival of La Paloma)*. The former deals with the struggles of two young lovers attempting to see each other in spite of parental objections. In the latter sainete, a work of large merit, a jealous young man discovers his competitor to be seventy years of age.

Ricardo de la Vega played a vital role in establishing the *género chico*. Two of his abbreviated sainetes without music, staged in 1875 and entitled *Providencias judiciales (Judicial Decisions)* and *Los baños del Manzanares (The Baths of the Manzanares)*, were heralded as prime movers of the new popular theater. Thirteen years later Vega began writing nothing but lyrical sainetes, one of the best being *La canción de la Lola (Lola's Song)*, which virtually ended the cultivation of the *zarzuela grande* and gave an impetus of distinction to the *género chico* that few pieces of the time could have managed.[41] *Lola's Song* was staged only three months after Arniches premièred his first play, *Publishing House*.

Arniches admired the works of Ricardo de la Vega. He employed much of the master's vivacity and local color in his early writings. His own success soon eclipsed that of the esteemed Vega, owing primarily to Arniches' youthful vitality as compared to the older playwright's waning creativity, and secondly to the fact that Arniches captivated the public's interest by adding to the established sentimental line of the musical sainete a conflict of love and justice in opposition to the forces of evil and dishonor. Arniches' writings concentrate more on the triumph of personal dignity, while Vega's portraits after 1888 continue to manifest the happy and carefree folk spirit of the epoch.

As one reads the texts of outstanding *género chico* plays of the late nineteenth century, it becomes evident that the decline of the movement came about as a result of an overabundance of shallow plots, an increase in musical compositions, overelaborate stage effects, and the ever-recurring insistence on stock theatrics and situations. In contrast to this trend toward nonliterary spectacles and public boredom, Arniches' early theater exalted the superiority of a weak figure over an apparently stronger force; he brought to the forefront an artistic defense for the kind of heroism that is achieved through sacrifice, hard work, and the cultivation of sound Christian values.

IX *The Quintero Brothers and Arniches*

The brothers Serafín (1871–1938) and Joaquín (1873–1944) Álvarez Quintero were prolific writers of gentle, often sentimental comedies. As was the case with Arniches, they too began their careers by writing light comediettas. Their first play was staged the same year that Arniches made his debut as a writer (1888). For fifty years they continued producing, and wrote more than two hundred charming, optimistic pieces whose mainstreams of inspiration were the Andalusian countryside and the genial, inoffensive inhabitants of Seville. Without exception, their sainetes celebrate the essential goodness of human nature. Such titles as *El patio (The Patio)* and *Las flores (Flowers)* have endeared their fresh playlets to theater groups worldwide. They exalted the beauty of Andalusia with the same devotion that Arniches showed for Madrid. Their names have become synonymous with the people and back streets of Seville, much in the same way that Pereda is associated with the Cantabrian Mountains, Blasco Ibáñez with the *huertas* of Valencia, and Gabriel y Galán with the wide plains of Extremadura. Theirs was a labor of love, re-creating in the clean and warmly human atmosphere of their sainetes the laughter and humor of the Mediterranean region.

One striking similarity in their writings with those of Carlos Arniches is the importance they assign to the female figure as the protagonist of many plays. With the emancipation of women following the Revolution of 1868, the woman's worth as a wife and mother is highly honored in Spanish literature. Whereas the wife and family were virtually ignored in many earlier sainetes and zarzuelas, their presence guides to a large extent the movement of the action in the writings of Arniches and the Quintero brothers. This active force is not analogous to the domineering and overpowering women in Jacinto Benavente's theater, nor to the puzzling and demonic women in García Lorca's plays. With few exceptions, the women of Arniches and the Quintero brothers are simple, honest, magnanimous, and sacrificing. Their goodness in the dramatic framework of a play is sensed even when the protagonists or dominant characters are men.

The Quintero brothers' work differs from that of Arniches in two essential respects. First, the Quinteros' language is always polished and correct, while in several instances the witty jokes of Arniches' sainetes are contrived and fall betimes into the category of rough and vulgar speech. Arniches uses hyperbole and metaphor to caricature language and people, while the Quintero brothers employ a language free of deformation. However, it tends on occasion to be somewhat banal owing to their all too cultivated and academic style.

A second difference lies in the fact that Arniches explores with care the didactic and moral lessons inherent in the content of his plays, while the Quintero brothers are satisfied to portray, as Azorín states, a surface "tone of gentle serenity."[42] Only beauty and wit are their focal concern. In Arniches' few sainetes of an Andalusian or Levantine scene, this difference is especially apparent.[43] In *Gazpacho andaluz (Andalusian Gazpacho),* for example, a play written in the Andalusian dialect, the author is more intent on offering good advice for a happy marriage than in merely depicting local color.

The simple life and the spontaneous dialogue encountered in the Álvarez Quintero sainetes compare favorably with the entertaining farces that Arniches wrote up to the turn of the century. Then, with the sudden shift in intellectual and social expressions emerging as a consequence of the Spanish-American War of 1898, Arniches' theater became more prescriptive and far less grounded in a linear preoccupation with verbal amusement for the sole purpose of entertaining his public. Unlike the Quintero brothers' later plays, Arniches' writings from this time on were more profound and his commitment to moral and social issues was more obvious.

X *The* Género Chico

The historical development of the *género chico* has been amply and ably treated by Marciano Zurita and José Deleito y Piñuela.[44] With regard to Arniches' involvement in its evolution, two of our ensuing chapters will address themselves to the subject. Our only concern at present is to indicate the heightened attention that the one-act farce received in Spain during a period in which the modern theater was vastly enriched by the reawakening toward a national tradition.

The last three decades of the nineteenth century represent "one of the most brilliant and glorious eras in the history of the Spanish theater, with regard to its dramatists, comedy writers, *saineteros,* composers, actors, and singers.[45] An outpouring of over fifteen hundred one-act plays inundated the entertainment world of Madrid. These abbreviated dramas were divided into several scenes, called *cuadros,* and were enhanced by and often dependent upon musical compositions of catchy tunes and witty, satirical, or comical language.

Skillful in their ability to incorporate the vernacular within a dramatic depiction of folk scenes, the authors of the *género chico*—so named because of the brevity and condensation of the playlets of the era, in contrast to the lengthy productions of the so-called *género grande*—portrayed with realism and understanding the loves and ambitions of the people who moved through the streets of Madrid. Nearly all of the *género chico* pieces were *costumbrista* writings, insofar as their aim was to capture, interpret, and recreate the local scene.

For Marciano Zurita the *género chico* embraced any one-act play, with or without music, provided the work was staged independently and lasted no more than one hour.[46] Zurita considers the youthful Tomás Luceño (1844–1931) to be the legitimate inaugurator of the genre. Luceño, at the age of twenty-five, staged his first sainete, *Cuadros al fresco (Open-Air Scenes),* in 1870, then followed that success with two other nonmusical hits, *El teatro moderno (The Modern Theater)* and *El arte por las nubes (Sky-High Art).* The immense popularity of these sainetes gave rise to a superabundance of farces written by a host of individuals, among them such illustrious figures as Miguel Echegaray, Miguel Ramos Carrión, Vital Aza, Javier de Burgos, José López Silva, Sinesio Delgado, Fernández Shaw, the aforenamed Ricardo de la Vega, and the man whose exquisite literary contributions lifted the genre to a height of true artistic dignity, Carlos Arniches.

The *género chico* occasioned an extraordinary response from the Spanish public, an emotional response that determined in the course of a few years an aesthetic and social awareness for the diverse levels, professions, and attitudes which characterized the Madrilenean society of the time. The *género chico* awakened a collective interest in a new era of music, song, dance, clever dialogue, and dynamic histrionics, prompting the citizenry of Madrid to respond with a high regard for theatrical entertainment. "Isn't it truly singular," wrote Rubén Darío in 1905, "that in this land of Quevedos and of Góngoras, the only innovators of the lyrical medium, the only liberators of rhythm, have been the poets of *Madrid Cómico* and the librettists of the *género chico?*"[47] The movement generated, in effect, a unique sense of social consciousness toward customs and conventions in the speech, behavior, sentiments, and lyrical expressions of the residents of the Spanish capital. It united people with that intoxicating kind of joy to which Julio Cejador y Frauca was referring when he praised the *género chico* for its "popular philosophy and elevated art."[48]

The social implications of this artistic phenomenon have not to our knowledge been fully examined. They appear worthy of serious study.[49] For the time being it might be stated that as in the era of Philip IV, when Lope de Vega's theater literally defined a new age with its seductive force, so in the latter part of the nineteenth century were the inhabitants of Madrid girded together in a fellowship of mutual understanding through art. The *género chico*'s proud achievement was the formation of an alliance between the stage and the street.

CHAPTER 3

Arniches as Collaborator

IN the course of forging his distinctly personal style and of master-
ing the technical skills that in time would come to be regarded
as a hallmark of his independent artistry, Carlos Arniches wrote
over sixty percent of his plays in collaboration with more than twenty
different playwrights. [1] Before his fortieth birthday, he had written
only eleven plays by his own hand, while sixty had been produced
in coauthorship with his many colleagues of the *género chico*
tradition.

Arniches' interest in seeking out talented individuals with whom
to share the labor of a theatrical production was not confined to his
youthful years of literary dependency. Even in his mature period he
consented to share his name and reputation with writers of much
less renown. As late as 1934, while approaching his sixty-eighth year
and having only recently completed the last of his celebrated grotesque tragedies, did he invite his aging friend Joaquín Abati to labor
conjointly with him in the writing of a new farce.

With characteristic modesty Arniches once observed that all of his
collaborators were superior to him in talent and aptitude. [2] Throughout his lifetime he regarded them with high esteem and respected
their competence, yet countered with firmness the charge by some
critics that he had exploited the craft of his friends in order to
broaden his own popularity. Shortly before he died, Arniches
affirmed that had he known how to exploit latent talent, he would
have exploited his own. [3]

I *The Art of Collaboration*

The history of the *género chico* is a chronicle of collective achievements. It was created by, and in its turn produced, a generation of
writers, composers, musicians, singers, actors, and promoters,
actuated and cheered by a vast entourage of grateful spectators and

48

enough hospitable critics to outweigh the grumblings of its few detractors. For more than forty years it was the predominant art form in Madrid drama. With several thousand productions to amuse its spectators, the genre was lifted by public response from the context of a popular pastime to the status of a national institution. The contributions of artists and playgoers alike formulated, in the words of Torrente Ballester, that period of literary history in which "the heart and soul of Spain were captured and expressed in word and song."[4]

In an era distinguished for artistic alliances and mutual influences, the dramatist who created exclusively in isolation was rare. Young playwrights tended to work together, seemingly unmindful of the risk of sacrificing unity of action and uniformity of style in their eagerness to build the fabric of a play on team effort. Nor did collaboration mean a simple give-and-take between two talented individuals; it involved the deliberations, inventiveness, and ingenuity of all people concerned with the production. Even the actors, the composers, and the musicians occasionally affected a profound influence on the creative process.

Fernando Vela writes that "an entire generation of writers and composers labored, as it were, as a team, with a continuity and solidarity rarely recorded. . . . If a composer wrote the music to the libretto for an author who later formed an alliance momentarily with another musician, the first composer, for his part, also went over to write music for another author. Partnerships were broken and remade constantly as if, and because of the fact that, the source from which their works proceeded was everyone's common property."[5]

Many writers of the *género chico* had grown accustomed to the notion of a literary partnership by writing for major newspapers of Madrid and Barcelona. This was clearly the case for Arniches who, as a reporter at the age of eighteen, was affiliated with a large staff of journalists for Barcelona's *La Vanguardia,* and later as an editor for Madrid's *El Diario Universal.* Occasional articles and humoristic sketches, written in concert with his co-workers, paved the way for more lucrative coalitions in dramaturgy. Arniches was not unlike many aspiring writers of his day, who accepted the practice of collaboration as a vocational norm and found that poverty could be deterred in the merging of several talents. Also contributing to the predilection for professional alliances was the widespread popularity of *tertulias*, which to this day attract large numbers of the intelligentsia and provide an outlet for individuals to give public expression to their opinions regarding art, literature, social problems, and politics. A *tertulia* is a social gathering in which topics of mutual interest to the group are enthusiastically discussed. In the long history of famous literary *tertulias*, the improvisation of ideas leading to the formulation of a work of art has often been the outgrowth of acquaintances fashioned in the tumult of a crowded, smoke-filled tavern, where not infrequently renowned artists have gathered to inspire their devotees with the verve of their creative thinking.

On a more formal level, the establishment in the 1890's of three distinct literary societies generated a sense of mutual interdependence among Spanish writers. These were *La Asociación Lírico-Dramática (The Lyric-Dramatic Association); La Sociedad de Autores, Compositores y Editores de Música (The Society of Authors, Composers, and Music Publishers)*, both of short-term duration; and the more robust *Sociedad de Autores Españoles (Society of Spanish Authors)*.

Intended as administrative offices to protect the rights of authors and to regulate financial concerns for all participants in artistic functions, these societies also afforded playwrights, scenarists, librettists, composers, and script editors a favorable center for professional conviviality. An author in search of qualified assistance for the writing or production of his play found in the associations a legal and remunerative means of contacting and contracting theater people for future engagements.

As a result of the universal spirit of cooperation that bound unskilled entertainers together with gifted artists, that produced an engaging array of trivia flanked by brilliant masterworks, that inundated the theater world with titillating banality leavened by occasional magnificence, the billboards of Spain displayed hundreds of names mated in partnership. Historically, the art of collaboration in the *género chico* began with the advent of the genre itself, in 1867, and continued with a frequency proportionate to the growth of light entertainment, reaching its apex in the partnership of the two men who best exemplified solidarity and productivity through literary collaboration: the brothers Joaquín and Serafín Álvarez Quintero. With Serafín's death in 1938, the *género chico* had run its course, and collaboration in the theater had likewise declined, only to be manifested occasionally but without substantial literary brilliance in the writing of musical revues and light comedies up to the present day.

II *Arniches and His Collaborators: The First Decade*

During his first ten years as a composer of the *género chico,* Carlos Arniches coauthored over thirty one-act plays in the zarzuela tradition. No one of them has achieved distinction. In their artistic creation and inner content, they are far inferior to those plays authored by him alone and they fall short as well of the quality of his later works of collaboration with Enrique García Álvarez. Through these early writings, however, Arniches worked out his own dramatic conception, testing the taste of his public and the response of his critics in a gradual shift from pieces of simple action, topical humor, and weak dialogue, to works of more complicated and interwoven intrigue, comedy of situation, and realistic speech. In time substance replaced frivolity, and a seriousness of purpose replaced the exciting novelty of making money.

In the main Arniches shared his decade of apprenticeship with two other novices of the theater, Gonzalo Cantó Vilaplana of Alicante and Celso Lucio López from Burgos. Arniches' first play, written at the age of twenty-one, was produced with the aid of the elder Cantó, who himself had published some mediocre poems, had witnessed with dismay the failure of his only drama, and was eager to prosper as a playwright. Following the box office success of their play, *Publishing House,* a musical satire on the degeneration of popular literary forms of the day, Arniches and Cantó wrote ten one-act plays together, premièred a three-act zarzuela, then abruptly severed their relationship in 1892 for reasons that have never been made public. Vicente Ramos speculates that the rupture came about for financial reasons.[6] It should also be restated that Arniches' brusque and nervous temperament in connection with the rehearsals and staging of his plays did not always endear him to his colleagues. Of more lasting and fruitful a duration was Arniches' partnership with Celso Lucio, with whom he wrote twenty-four plays between 1889 and 1900. As was the case with Cantó, Arniches produced for the most part one-act zarzuelas with Lucio, manifesting no apparent shift in design or dramatic technique. In the year 1900 Celso Lucio was stricken with hemiplegia and was forced to retire from active playwriting for the remainder of his life.

Arniches' writings of collaboration with Cantó and Lucio were imitative extensions of the kind of colorful musical variety pieces already made popular by such celebrated masters of the *género chico* as Ricardo de la Vega, Javier de Burgos, and Ramos Carrión. In this respect, the plays which emerged from his ten-year period initiation into dramaturgy do little more than perpetuate a rich tradition that had begun three centuries earlier in the lively pasos of Lope de Rueda, extending into modern times by way of the sainetes of Ramón de la Cruz.

Aside from strengthening his reputation as an able and well-received playwright, Arniches' early works add no new perspectives to the genre. Viewed in their totality, his characters are often coined in a common mold. They are involved in single, uncomplicated love conflicts which almost always end happily. Comical scenes and comical situations are repeated in different plays. Clever tricks and surprising side effects are calculated to elicit applause and laughter, while action and dialogue are reduced to a level of secondary importance. The plot line in most of these works is based primarily on mistaken identities and hilarious misunderstandings. The prevalent themes are jealousy and rivalry born of love. Fashionable jokes, beatings, and the always present gaiety of song and dance add a touch of vaudeville to the charm of colloquial expressions and local color.

Despite the levity and froth, there are two important elements worthy of comment in Arniches' writings with Cantó and Lucio, and both seem strongly suggestive of Arniches' dominant influence on the labors of his colleagues. The first point to be considered is the occasional emergence of a spontaneous, sparkling dialogue, albeit subordinated to the surface stage action. This ingredient, brought to greater prominence in plays written by him alone during this same period of time, is a mere prototype in embryo for the splendor of his later plays, and contributes here to charge the atmosphere with a sense of reality and to keep the writings from degenerating into banal farces.

The second important component is the emphasis on problems of real people extracted from folk background: peddlers, washerwomen, barbers, dressmakers, maids—in short, the poor and simple citizens in the city. With each consecutive play, Arniches seems to be moving more and more into a detailed glorification of Madrid, seeking to embody the heart and soul of Spain in the laughter and tears of her humble and hard-working people. While characterization is not strong in these early folk pieces, the intent to dramatize small love tales and petty sufferings lifted from a panoramic tableau of urban life is unmistakable, and in time becomes paramount to the central purpose in all of Arniches' better dramas.

III *Arniches and Enrique García Álvarez*

On the evening of February 9, 1888, in Madrid's Eslava Theater, a young boy of fifteen witnessed the première of Carlos Arniches' first play. His enthusiasm for the work stirred anew his passion for the theater and instilled in the youngster's mind a deep sense of allegiance to the playwright with whom some eleven years later he would begin a sixteen-year period of assiduous and fruitful collaboration.

While still in his teens, the boy began his productive career, joining the even younger Antonio Paso to write twenty-five plays for the *género chico*. Between 1897 and 1912 he collaborated almost exclusively with Arniches, writing twenty-five more plays, then joined Pedro Muñoz Seca, Antonio Casero, Joaquín Abati, and many more. He became renowned as one of Spain's most successful and most indefatigable collaborators. He rarely wrote a play without the aid of a coauthor.

Enrique García Álvarez (1873–1931) occupies a unique position in the development of dramatic humor. Sharing over one hundred titles with some twelve other playwrights, he is the acknowledged creator of a new genre in the Spanish theater, a comic prescription that bears the name *astracán* (astrakhan).[7] Because he is always associated with some one among several playwrights, his personal role in the development of the contemporary theater of humor has been greatly underrated and merits a serious revaluation.

The drama critic Alfredo Marquerie refers to García Álvarez as a writer of "fecund talent, a true giant of popular humor."[8] With this observation, Marquerie restates the titles that José Casado gave García Álvarez a quarter of a century earlier: "The King of Wit, The Prince Heir of Jest, The Emperor of Charm."[9] Miguel Mihura, one of Spain's most celebrated contemporary dramatists,

mentions him first and foremost among the authors whose talent
determined the ultimate appearance of a new kind of dramatic
humor in Spain.[10] Enrique Jardiel Poncela also extols his importance in a tribute that singles him out as having inspired a direction so
entirely new that it established its own precedent: "García Álvarez
influenced, changed, and excited those writers who already possessed
a distinct literary manner; he guided, oriented, and gave life to those
who had not yet attained a full personal style; . . . he inaugurated a
violent, grotesque, fantastic, and marvelously absurd form of
comedy for the theater, without antecedents in Spain or elsewhere."[11]

Jardiel's favorable opinion of García Álvarez is also supported
by the contemporary playwright Alfonso Paso, who mentions
Enrique García Álvarez' name as heading an illustrious company of
comic writers. They include Carlos Arniches, Pedro Muñoz Seca,
Joaquín Abati, and Paso's own father, Antonio, and represent
"The Comic Generation of 1898," the generation which revolu-
tionized theatrical situations, dialogues, and theses; the generation
responsible for creating the *género chico,* that enlarged the sainete,
that gave intense life to the zarzuela, and of which Azorín ventured
to say that if the group had been born in France, it would now be
honored in marble and crowned with laurel in the Champs Elysées.[12]

Carlos Arniches, for his part, found in García Álvarez a kindred
spirit possessing qualities of character and talent which complemented his own. "That which didn't occur to the one," writes
Zurita, "occurred to the other. If a witty line got by Arniches, García
Álvarez picked it up. And more than witty sayings, which did indeed
abound, they also exploited comic situations. In this connection
there has never been anyone to compare with them . . ."[13]

Arniches benefited particularly from García Álvarez' enormous
capacity for sustaining a sense of charm and comedy throughout
an involved situation. Heretofore Arniches had written plays with
simple plots, limited complications, and a linear development.
Hereafter his writings are to reflect a new dimension of complexity,
with ingenious subplots bound coherently to the entangled affairs
of a lengthier and more compelling main action. Zurita is correct
in his assertion that in this partnership Arniches enters a new, mature
phase of his artistic development.[14] The plays he wrote with García
Álvarez differ significantly from those of the preceding decade: they
reveal an expansion of inner content, a heightened sense of comedy,

and a more pronounced inventiveness of creative language, bringing dialogue to the foreground to share a role equal to that of the comic situation. Moreover, the prominence of dialogue now serves to enhance characterization, adding depth and dimension to the delineation of simple folk types who formerly were drawn from an urban mold.

The year 1912 marked the end of the literary collaboration and friendship between Arniches and García Álvarez. A rupture due to personal friction quickly became a subject for public talebearing. Local newspapers publicized the dispute, critics took sides, and the breach was widened. Vicente Ramos, who leans strongly to the side of Arniches, affirms that the rift between the two men proved beneficial to the Alicantine playwright who, upon finding himself alone, "continued to unfold and to widen his personal and glorious artistic pathway," notwithstanding the agony that attended his falling-out with an old friend and that even resulted in a prolonged physical illness.[15]

García Álvarez turned to the eminent playwright, Pedro Muñoz Seca, with whom he labored for several years, developing his *astracán* humor from the moderate use of dialogue which characterized his plays with Arniches into the most lavish exhibition of vocalized inverisimilitude and absurdity to be witnessed on the Spanish stage.[16] It is during this period that Muñoz Seca reigned supreme as the chief architect of the *astracán,* producing with notable technical skill that which Valbuena Prat labels "a theater of absolute absurdity, of total jest."[17]

García Álvarez' work was concluded with his death in 1931, thus ending what Mihura has called "the most extraordinary case of vagrancy in the modern theater," referring to the man's incessant collaboration and boundless energy.[18] Mihura valued the importance of this exceptional personality to such an extent as to assign to him a kind of patriarchal role in the development of his own and others' dramatic efforts. In 1943 he wrote of García Álvarez as "the author whom I have most admired in my youth, the most nonsensical, the least bourgeois, perhaps the master of those of us who afterwards began to cultivate a theater of the absurd."[19] García Alvarez' natural gift of comedy left his many co-authors better writers for having worked with him.

IV *The* Fresco *Era*

The innovative elements that Arniches and García Álvarez brought to the stage—plot entanglements, humor through dialogue, and character development—converge in the writings of their best-known comedies, the *fresco* ("rapscallion") plays, five one-act musicals written between 1903 and 1912; and the delightful and highly praised one-act lyrical comedy entitled *Alma de Dios (The Kindhearted Woman)*, premièred in 1907. Of the twenty-five plays they wrote together, these six works would suffice to justify the literary importance of their collaboration.

The *fresco* is a roguish, teasing fellow in whom is combined the cunning of the *pícaro* and the disarming wit of the fool. In the writings of Arniches and García Álvarez, he is the incarnation of deceit, gaiety, cowardice, carelessness, and greed all rolled up in a character whose devious actions miscarry. He must therefore suffer the consequences of his intemperance at the hands of a rigid, outraged society. Berenguer reduces the *fresco*'s indulgence in vice to "the exploitation of two capital sins: lust and gluttony."[20] For these moral deviations he is punished in a physical way through beatings, fisticuffs, or clubbings.

The *fresco* is a dreg of society, an antihero, whose slyness and outward optimism hide a pervasive cowardice, and whose malefactions are representative of the emergence of debilitating influences in the Spanish social environment, namely, a weakening of individual integrity, a disregard for honest work, and a relaxation of moral scruples. Critics have been all too prone to dismiss the *fresco* plays as aimless slapstick, viewing the corporal punishment dealt the offender as contrived farce patterned after Rueda's pasos, the Italian *commedia dell'arte* and the hilarious endings of Molière's plays. While all of the inanity of low comedy is indeed present, and thus earmarks the genre as a legitimate product of its time, there is an unmistakable didactic intention underlying the portrayal of the *fresco*'s extravagant conduct, a characteristic of significant importance to the evolution of Arniches' theater.

The first *fresco* play, entitled *El terrible Pérez (Terrible Pérez)*, appeared in 1903, less than two months after Benavente had premièred his masterpiece, *La noche del sábado (The Witches' Sabbath)*. Pérez is a laughable and frustrated Don Juan figure who attempts to woo a married woman. He overrates his seductive powers and falls victim in the end to a furious cudgelling at the hands of a pack of deceived husbands. A winsome and witty dialogue upholds the play's jocundity and accounts in large measure for the impression of comic absurdity surrounding the action. This same ingredient is what contributes to the subsequent rise of the notion of *astracán* humor, or the kind of illogical exercise with common speech that Torrente Ballester labels "language twisting" and deplores as an unhealthy symptom of the degradation of dramatic literature.[21] It is this element which suggests García Álvarez' role in the play's construction, inasmuch as the absurdist tendency was virtually abandoned by Arniches when the two men parted company, but it was picked up, intensified, and perpetuated by Pedro Muñoz Seca when García Álvarez shifted over to his camp as a devoted collaborator.

Retribution for indiscreet acts is likewise the theme for the second *fresco* play, staged one year later, in July of 1904. Vicente Ramos states that this work, entitled *El pobre Valbuena (Poor Valbuena)*, enjoyed a much greater success than *Terrible Pérez* and did in fact occasion a kind of collective hysteria in the audience, "resulting in illnesses caused by too much laughter."[22] The humor originates once again from a concatenation of unbelievable events surrounding an artful rascal, Valbuena, whose strange repertory of talents includes crime writing, cricket cage building, guitar instruction, perfume concocting, and training blackbirds in fifteen lessons, and who adds trickery to his skills by attempting to snare women into his embrace with feigned epileptic seizures. Valbuena's rival is the jealous lover, Pepe the Tranquil, whose nickname would suggest a subdued and pleasant nature, though his true colors are quite apparent when he administers a tremendous beating to Valbuena in the final scene.

A sense of human tenderness and pathos envelops the action of the third *fresco* play, *El iluso Cañizares (Deluded Cañizares)*, 1905. Unlike his two predecessors, Aquilino Cañizares does not exercise his mischievousness in the affairs of love, but turns instead to political aspirations. Imbued with redemptive reform measures of socialism, he dreams his way, in Walter Mitty fashion, into the governorship of Madrid. Then, like Sancho Panza realizing the long-awaited ideal, he too is handed the scepter of authority. But from this point on his life crumbles into wretchedness. He finds the tasks of his office insurmountable, his wife and children become corrupted and vain, attempts are made on his life, and he loses the joy and serenity which accompanied his former existence as a dreamer and common laborer. *Deluded Cañizares* offers a distinct fore-shadowing of Arniches' thematic concentration on the simplicity of human tasks and feelings, as portrayed in many of his later sainetes, comedies, tragicomedies, and the grotesque tragedies. The difference here is that the simple and harmless protagonist is a pitiful creature whose ineptitude is the product of idleness and ignorance, while in later plays the featured characters are more sympathetically drawn and display convincing psychological conflicts in their struggles to achieve positive heroism.

El pollo Tejada (Shrewd Tejada) is the fourth in the series of the "rapscallion" comedies. The authors labeled their new musical a "comic-lyric adventure" and designed its frivolous numbers for sheer public delight. The shameless protagonist, now sixty years of age, is once again overly fond of women and, as was the case with Pérez and Valbuena before him, he overleaps propriety by presuming to court another man's wife. He escapes physical harm by wafting heavenward in a balloon, only to land amidst an African harem. The play is pure nonsense, but does afford its authors a chance to develop their sustained caricature of a Don Juan figure in picaresque attire.

El fresco de Goya (Rascally Goya) is the final comic treatment of the *fresco* type. The play was staged only one month before the breach of friendship occurred between Arniches and García Álvarez. If they possibly envisioned another play in this tradition, the notion floundered and was quickly forgotten in the wake of their irreparable misunderstanding.

The six years that separate *Rascally Goya* from the inane farce about Tejada served to temper the delineation of the *fresco* along more sophisticated lines. *Rascally Goya* is a more mature and well-devised work. In it the playwrights ridicule the antics of Paco Goya, a married man with an incurable appetite for women. Using the promise of marriage as his bait, Paco lures attractive young ladies into lovemaking. The deception is revealed, of course, and the inevitable punishment is meted out.

Pérez, Valbuena, Cañizares, Tejada, and Goya, among other *fresco* types that make an appearance in less important zarzuelas by Arniches and García Álvarez, share in common some of the traditional traits of conduct usually associated with the *pícaro*. Each protagonist emerges as a poor and needy loafer living by his wits and trickery in the popular quarters of Madrid. Neither is sorry about his bad deeds, and on the surface displays no fear with regard to the outcome of his chicanery. With the exception of Cañizares, whose duplicity follows a political line, each one of the disreputable but still lovable rogues is propelled by lust and material greed, and each one's sin is expiated by means of corporal punishment at the hands of a competent adversary. Unlike the *picaro* of the Golden Age, the *fresco* is a mature if not married man, and rather than shifting from one master to another, his extravagant meanderings take him from mistress to mistress. He is, nonetheless, as Ruiz Morcuende states, "a worthy successor of Buscón and of Guzmán de Alfarache," having jumped from the novel to the theater with a new appellation.[23]

In a recent essay on the creative genius of Arniches, José Bergamín observes that that which is original, that which is truly new in each variation on the same theme in the *fresco* series, is "the expressive force, the dramatic skill, the clear-sighted and vivid observation incarnated in all and each one" of these colorful theatrical figures, "and all because of the marvelous inventiveness of creative language."[24] This comment is most perceptive, in view of the importance attributed to dialogue as the dramatic force underlying Arniches' later focus on the tenderness, vigor, and drama of the human personality. The *fresco* plays represent, therefore, the first major step in the development of an authentic dramatic technique. They likewise constitute an introductory phase in the evolvement of a strong moral and social criticism, one of the hallmarks of Arniches' later plays.

Granted, the appearance of a concrete moral lesson is not an ostensible intention in the *fresco* plays. It rather emerges in a logical and sequential manner from the unfolding of a comical human experience. As Berenguer writes, "the art of the great playwright consists in restraining the didactic solution, that it not be a motif forced from the theme, but that it issue forth as a sudden, fluent, and inevitable result of the execution of events."[25] Finally, the *fresco* era is significant in that it represents a departure point for Arniches' thematic emphasis on the down-and-out ne'er-do-wells of Madrilenean society. The *fresco* is a forerunner to the *chulo,* or low-class rascal, of his later sainetes and comedies, and to the roguish protagonists of his celebrated grotesque tragedies.

V Alma de Dios (The Kindhearted Woman)

Heralded in its day a master example of a sainete and praised by Ramón del Valle-Inclán as being his favorite from among all the works written for the *género chico,* this one-act lyrical comedy was first performed shortly before Christmas of 1907, eight days after Benavente premièred his great philosophical-moral satire, *Los intereses creados (The Bonds of Interest).*

The Kindhearted Woman enjoyed a remarkable success in Madrid, remaining on the boards longer than any theater production of the season and accumulating a record of over seven hundred performances by 1919.[25] During the first few months of its inaugural staging, the demand for tickets was so great that opportunistic vendors were able to resell orchestra seats for two and three times their original value.[27] According to Fernández Almagro, it was "the favorite play of the theater of its time."[28]

Much of the play's beauty and popularity can be attributed to its inspired music, provided by José Serrano Simeón, who composed songs and melodies for twelve of Arniches' zarzuelas and musical sainetes.[29] Aside from its lovely music, the play is itself an amusing melodrama, well structured, and written with a strong sensitivity for the emotional response of the audience.

Its action surrounds the vicissitudes of a defamed but innocent orphan girl named Eloísa. Accused of giving birth to an illegitimate child, Eloísa is ill treated by her employer and loses for a time the respect and attentions of Matías, her boyfriend. She finds comfort in the arms of Matías' aunt, the kind and righteously indignant Ezequiela. Good Aunt Ezequiela, convinced of Eloísa's innocence, invites everyone involved in the scandal to attend the baptism of the child in question. Meanwhile, angered over mounting accusations with respect to her honor, Eloísa consigns the child to Irene, a woman who happens to be its real mother. The persistent Ezequiela, tracking the child's whereabouts, discovers the truth, brings about a happy ending, and pronounces the moral lesson of the play: "The goodness of others should be of consequence to all."

For Marciano Zurita this charming playlet was conclusive proof of García Álvarez' influence over Arniches, owing to the vaudevillian atmosphere in the sacristy scene.[30] Vicente Ramos differs with this point of view, maintaining that Arniches' influence appears ostensibly in the fundamental moral intent of the sainete as well as in its development.[31] This disagreement might easily be resolved by suggesting that both critics are correct in their respective arguments. Arniches' influence is especially evident in the technical precision, the psychological observations, and the didactic design inherent in the dramatic action, while García Álvarez' influence dominates with respect to the verve and richness of the humor and the energetic dialogue of the play. The combination of these virtues produced a play of excellent craftsmanship. *The Kindhearted Woman* is perhaps the best work that Arniches wrote as a collaborator.

CHAPTER 4

"The Illustrious Sainetero"

W HY is Carlos Arniches such an important figure in the history of the Spanish theater? In order to give credit to the dual role that Arniches played as both the developer of one art form and the innovator of another, the answer to this question requires a two-part statement: Early in his career he perfected the classical Spanish sainete and became its most distinguished architect; late in life he added a new and exciting genre to the tradition of full-length drama: the grotesque tragedy. For either of these achievements his reputation will endure.

It is our present task to examine the merits embodied in the title conferred upon Arniches while he was still in his early thirties, namely, that of "King of the Sainete."[1] Only as we understand the nature of his contributions to the theater of that time will we perceive the significance of his fame as the acknowledged master of that form of the *género chico* which, as Pedro Salinas observed, brought Spanish realism to its greatest height.[2]

Having defined the term sainete and discussed even though sketchily its historical development in Spanish literature, our main concern now is to focus attention directly on the substance and intent of some sainetes which Arniches wrote unaided during his highly productive life. It will be of interest to select for discussion several exemplary sainetes from different stages of the author's career, thus enabling us to point to a remarkable maturing process and to note the playwright's shift from festive *costumbrista* pieces to a concern for the moral and social conscience of his fellow men.

I El santo de la Isidra (Isidra's Saint)

Had Arniches been swayed by the public response accorded *Isidra's Saint,* this first sainete by him as an independent playwright might never have been performed a second time. On the night of its première, the play seemed destined for oblivion. It was rejected with vociferous cries, footstamping, and incessant heckling.[3]

Then, in a manner explicable only to veterans of the study of human nature, the play suddenly caught on. Within a month it was scheduled for daily performances on a double bill with another success of the *género chico, La revoltosa (The Mischievous Lass),* by López Silva and Fernández Shaw and premièred three months earlier. The two sainetes have since become favorites for return engagements in the Spanish capital.

Briefly summarized, the plot is as follows: Isidra, the lovely heroine of the play, is named after the Patron Saint of the City and Court of Madrid, whose festive day falls in mid-May and is celebrated with dancing, food, and song. Amid preparations for the joyous event, an engaging love conflict begins to unfold. Isidra has recently broken her engagement to the deceitful Epifanio, a boisterous, boastful bully who has sworn vengeance on his estranged sweetheart by intimidating all would-be suitors who show any sign of interest in the available girl. Into the fray walks Venancio, a poor and modest baker, whose timidity before women leaves him forlorn, weak, and tongue-tied. Venancio pledges his intention to dance with Isidra at the outset of the picnic celebration that afternoon, contrary to Epifanio's threat on his well-being and in response to Isidra's own declaration that "a man who keeps silent is good for nothing."

The scene shifts from the lively street of Old Madrid to the showdown on the San Isidro Meadow. As the atmosphere sparkles with improvised singing, good-natured disputes, and the fever of a long-anticipated fiesta, Venancio exasperates his rival by daring to dance with Isidra. The play ends in the inevitable brawl that finds the cowardly Epifanio scurrying away in the wake of a convincing display of valor on the part of the shy and gentle Venancio.

A play written about the annual San Isidro Festival was not unique to the Spanish theater. Lope de Vega, Hurtado de Mendoza, Ramón de la Cruz, and Miguel Echegaray had each written plays on this subject. Thematically, *Isidra's Saint* also has a precedent in Javier de Burgos' excellent sainete, *Los valientes (The Bullies),* staged thirty-two years earlier. In Burgos' treatment a fierce barkeeper intimidates an entire town with his bullying, only to see his arrogance crumble before the sudden courage of his daughter's bashful but indignant suitor. The similarity between the two plays is not surprising, in that Arniches at this early period as *sainetero* relies on many commonplace formulas of the *género chico.*

The originality of *Isidra's Saint* lies elsewhere than in its thematic treatment. Its major importance is found in the magnificent local color attending the fast pace of the action. The plot itself is of little significance to the enduring quality of the piece; what stands out is its enlivened atmosphere magnified by the presence of multitudes in constant activity. The opening scene, for example, is an unusual achievement of sustained animation. It is structured to convey a sense of the unrehearsed spirit of living, to involve the audience in the delights of a seemingly impromptu expression. Flower vendors are shouting, a shoemaker is pounding, two young people are arguing, and other movements and sounds charge the festive climate with that special element of picturesque charm the Spanish call *costumbrismo*.

It is this element—the color, pageantry, and emphasis on a folk tradition—which has endeared Arniches to a grateful Spanish public. His work—and *Isidra's Saint* is one of the best examples— is an admixture of a native provincial wit and vivacity that, as an Alicantian, he came by honestly, and the characteristic spontaneity of life in the capital which he absorbed by way of his voluntary adoption of Madrid. The vitality of the play's first part is amplified in later scenes, reaching a climax in the gaiety of the gathering on the San Isidro Meadow, a playground for Madrilenean society where swings, picnic tables, trinket stands, and many bustling, laughing, flirting people fill the framework of the action. It is here that we reencounter in dramatic form the same beautiful world immortalized a century earlier in the bucolic paintings of Goya, who depicted on canvas the delights and the grace of the May 15th meadow retreat. Goya's vision of "La pradera de San Isidro" ("The Grassland of San Isidro") is a worthy companion to the playwright's sketch. Though it depicts aristocrats at play rather than the lowerclass subjects of Arniches' scene, it still conveys the freshness, light, color, and delicacy of handling that make Goya's achievement a direct source of inspiration for the testimony of joy documented in Arniches' charming sainete. Reportedly, Arniches went often to the Prado Museum to admire Goya's paintings, an experience which could not help but leave an impression with him that is strongly reflected in several of his plays.[4]

Another element important to the play is the delineation of the clean-cut, upstanding Venancio, who becomes in a figurative sense Isidra's saint, in answer to her lament: "Oh, I am choked by gall and fury in knowing I have no one to defend me." Venancio exemplifies the typical idealized hero of Arniches' early plays; that is, the virile young man who defends the principles of law, order, and justice. Many years after the creation of this figure, Arniches remarked that in his conception of Venancio he had attempted to embody the folk spirit of Spain: "Venancio is an honest, noble, and virtuous man. He is my concept of the expression of the common soul. He sums up all humble, noble, and industrious types."[5] These elements, says Pedro Salinas, though they converge here to form an admired hero in contrast to the rascally villain Epifanio, "have been the invariable ingredients of the genre for a long time, though with numerous differences; but at no time have they been managed with the same good fortune and precision as controlled by Arniches in this sainete."[6]

Venancio also foretokens a memorable character portrayal in one of Arniches' grotesque tragedies, that of Don Antonio in *Es mi hombre (That's My Man)*. In the later drama the hero struggles to overcome an inborn lack of courage and finds strength to fulfill his duty when the life and honor of his daughter are at stake. In both plays intimidation is used as a tool to control the actions of other men, and in each case the protagonist surmounts an instinctive fear in his pursuit for self-fulfillment. Arniches explores several variations on this theme in a number of his plays.

II Las estrellas (The Stars)

In the six years that intervene between the cheerful glorification of the San Isidro folk festival and the highly acclaimed sainete, *The Stars,* Arniches wrote twenty-four additional plays, three fourths of them in collaboration. This is the period in which Arniches' theater begins a gradual transformation from the genial vignettes of Madrid folklife to plays of an expanded intrigue dealing with life in that city. With the writing of *The Stars,* Arniches ventures into a realm of urgency, in which the appearance of social and moral concerns takes precedence over mere *costumbrismo.* So important is this step to his career, that in later years Arniches acknowledged the fact that *The Stars* and *That's My Man* were the two most representative works of his theater.[7]

The Stars is an admirable study on the time-honored theme of illusion versus reality. The barber Prudencio has two teen-age children, Casildo and Antoñita, of whom he is so profoundly fond that

he "becomes blind to their faults and sees things that just aren't so."
Impelled by the example of his friend Pepe, whose own wife and
daughter are reportedly making their fortune in Paris as members
of a successful dance troupe, Prudencio resolves to launch his
children on a quick trek to stardom. He intends to fashion Casildo,
a vain lad convinced of his own invincible power over the bulls,
into "the greatest bullfighter of the future and for all time." As for
Antoñita, who in truth has "less grace than a box of shoe polish,"
only a success of first magnitude on the stages of Europe will
satisfy her visionary father. Despite their awareness that Casildo
and Antoñita have no talent whatsoever, Prudencio's friends add
fuel to the barber's fantasies, urging, as Sancho urged Don Quijote,
the implementation of his idealistic plans. The children are themselves firm believers in their imminent conquests and prosperity.

In contrast with the irrational Prudencio is the practical and
realistic Feliciana, his strong-willed wife. Her efforts to put an end
to her husband's unbridled imaginings have little effect, however.
Learning that he had transferred the deed to the barber shop for only
seven hundred pesetas in order to buy Antoñita her debut in a local
music hall show, the prudent Feliciana confronts her three idealists
with an outburst of fury. She cuts off Casildo's revered queue,
rebukes her daughter into submission, and scorns the impossible
dreams of her husband. The upshot of the dispute is a voluntary
parting of ways. Prudencio leads his children out of the door and
into the world of fame and fortune. Feliciana must now enlist the
aid of her brother, an attorney, to invalidate the transfer of the deed.
As Part One closes, she finds herself alone, sole proprietor of a
barber shop, abandoned by her scatterbrained family.

In the second part of this one-act sainete we witness the heart-
rending downfall of Antoñita, whose radiant joy disintegrates
before the hissing, stamping, and shouting of an enraged audience,
now cognizant of her lack of talent:

> (*Tearful, choking, and without knowing what she is doing, she stops
> singing and shouts towards the public:*) —— You indecent —— ! *(Dread-
> ful clamor, shouts, imprecations. The curtain falls. Weeping grievously,
> she embraces Prudencio.)* —— Ay, my dear father, I believe they didn't
> like me!

Antoñita's humiliation is matched the same day by Casildo's
agonizing defeat with his first bull. He had lasted only a moment

before being tossed to the ground. With the help of a friend, he stumbled homeward, a broken and embittered young man.

The play ends with a typical but magnificent scene of reconciliation. Feliciana, whom Prudencio believed to be at home in bed indifferent to their fate, has been walking the streets in an agitated state, her heart bursting with remorse and love for her family. She encounters the three disillusioned runaways, now "cured of their insanity." Following her outburst of fury upon seeing them, she tenderly guides her husband and children into their home: "Go on, go into that corner of the house that you called foreboding and gloomy, because, you poor fools, you didn't know that it is through affection and work that we gain true joy and happiness."

The lesson is obvious, as Arniches meant it to be, and as is the case with most of his plays, the female figure reaffirms the moral truth. In this play the didactic intent is an eloquent foreshadowing of the deeper meanings contained in the later grotesque tragedies.

Not all is bromide in *The Stars,* however. Indeed, we note for the first time in Carlos Arniches' theater the emergence of subtle moral issues, of veiled social satire and suggestive irony, elements that have also begun to appear in his writings of collaboration with Enrique García Álvarez of this same period. And these are the elements that manifest a side of Arniches too often ignored by those who extol only his breezy little plays about folk customs. Arniches is an author of provocative innuendos, of subtle nuances that lightly skirt the edge of cynicism, only to spring back to provoke a knowing smile or to incite hearty laughter. In this play the words of the secondary figure, Pepe, reveal the moral tendency.

Pepe, it will be recalled, stirs up Prudencio's greed for fame and fortune by citing the recent triumph of his wife and daughter in the Parisian entertainment world. He does so in a spirit reminiscent of the criticism fashionable in the era of this play: "I have counseled him to sell everything, to leave this worthless Spain, to emigrate with his daughter to Paris as I will, for I'm going day after tomorrow. And in a couple of years we'll all return from abroad and—you know those big manors over on Lista Street, just beyond that cigar store there?—well, they'll be our hotels!" The pathos underlying this kind of quixotic thinking is made doubly poignant and personally tragic when we learn from Pepe at the end of the play, upon his return from Paris, that the money his wife and daughter had been amassing there was earned by prostitution.

The play does end on a typically happy note, "with abundant gladness because it signifies an affinity of extremes: the fusion of opposing optimisms, resulting in a pact of new life."[8] The "opposing optimisms" of which Berenguer speaks refer to, first, the vaulting idealism of Prudencio, the Don Quijote figure; and second, to the prudent aspirations of his wife, in a kind of Sancho Panza role. "It is in this respect a complete play, made up of the myth and the material of Alonso Quijano."[9]

III Del Madrid castizo (From the Soul of Madrid)

Arniches had reached a pinnacle of professional esteem and public acclaim when this series of popular dialogues he labeled *sainetes rápidos* (rapid sainetes) was published. Previously, at the insistence of Torcuato Luca de Tena, director of the widely circulated periodical *Blanco y Negro,* Arniches had written the eleven sainetes that comprise this collection solely for reading pleasure. Then, responding to popular demands, he gathered them from among the issues of *Blanco y Negro* and published the sketches under the title *Del Madrid castizo (From the Soul of Madrid)* in 1917.

Since Arniches' death, a few of these sainetes, incorrectly considered by some critics as being nonperformable, have been staged. Some have appeared as occasional entremeses between the acts of major comedies, as was the traditional practice with this abbreviated art form several centuries ago; others have been produced in a more formal manner, as was the case in 1952 with the creditable performance in Madrid's María Guerrero Theater of the special tribute to Arniches entitled *Fantasía 1900.*

We include at this juncture a general discussion of these absorbing "closet dramas" because they exhibit, in the words of Vicente Ramos, "a most notable moralizing intent, consistent with all of Arniches' theater and very much in line with the regenerational literature of the beginning of our century. Arniches not only captured the charming and amusing slang of Madrilenean poor districts, but, on an equal scale, he defined the concept of life, the simple yet profound ideology, of the people who inhabit those quarters."[10]

A topical outline of the sum and substance of each of these "rapid sainetes" will suffice to manifest the critical and satirical tone of the complete collection.

Los pobres (The Paupers) looks into "the filthy corners of a lamentable and miserable, insidious and sneaky Madrid," revealing the attitudes of the street beggars, the performance of their scurvy tricks, and their ironic sense of gratitude toward those who give alms, for without their generosity, the beggars would be forced to go to work.

Los culpables (The Guilty) concerns a heated argument in an open-air barber shop. Several men dispute the national prostration of Spain. In answer to the allegation that the bullfight is a blight corroding the nation, the principal interlocutor counters by saying that "the national ruin lies not in the bulls nor in the bullfighters, but in the people," and he accuses the working class of laziness and abulia. This point is endorsed by another participant who offers the following recipe for saving the country: "For ten years everyone will work and no one will talk. And after this term of application and silence, if we haven't progressed a thousand times over, I'll lay a wager on the notion that the whole encephalic mass will crush itself."

El premio de Nicanor (Nicanor's Prize) levels a harsh criticism at the lottery game which "in addition to consuming the daily wage of the poor people and leading them to ruin, produces nothing but sorrow."

Los neutrales (The Neutrals) presents three laborers debating the senselessness of war and the advantage of remaining neutral between Germany and the Allies. They find this dilemma easily resolved with the aid of a good bottle of wine.

El zapatero filósofo (The Philosophic Cobbler) deals with a New Year's Eve discussion between a quarrelsome old couple and their aging friend, who pose the problem of the absurdity of trying to change one's personal bad habits in the face of the unalterable fact that Spain is immured in a political, economic, and domestic decadence.

Los pasionales (The Impassioned) attacks both the inequity of court trials in which bribery and feigned emotion are rewarded, and the rascality of two boys who speak of taking physical vengeance on their girl friends for having spurned them. The one lad was successful; the other is attacked by a group of infuriated females who leave him beaten and humiliated for the police to lead away.

La risa del pueblo (The Laughter of the People) is an engrossing dramatization of the human penchant for ridiculing the foibles of others and enjoying their failure. The main character, Bonifacio, labels this warped sense of pleasure "barbarous and bestial behavior," then becomes in the end a party to the same moral deviation.

La pareja científica (The Scientific Couple) is a tender Christmas Eve tale of deep human pathos. Its theme is the dehumanizing nature of industrialization. Two police guards debate the validity of phrenology as a scientific gauge for determining criminal tendencies. Attempting to apply their theory to a real case, they interview a forlorn petty thief. He relates the story of his life, and they realize that hunger and privation have given rise to his crimes, that the blame for his indiscretions really rests with Spanish society.

Los ateos (The Atheists) suggests that even the most confirmed disbelievers cherish a sense of faith in a divine power. Floro, ridiculed in a tavern for having tipped his cap at the passing of a funeral coach, is a later witness to his atheistic scoffer's deep-seated conviction that all men owe God an expression of gratitude. The atheist declares: "When a man is well and healthy and finds himself in a tavern surrounded by four fools who will sneer at anything, that man is strong; he'll dare to challenge all that's human and all that's divine. But when the wind changes and the dark hour comes, and pain makes him frightened and he's all alone in a corner of his house, . . . regardless of his impiety, that man, I tell you, will raise his eyes to heaven and plead for mercy."

Los ricos (The Wealthy) depicts man's idealistic yearning for betterment in conflict with his basic egoism. Serapio, a carriage driver, conjectures that if he were only rich, he would share his money unselfishly with a needy world. Concluding this eloquent proclamation, he indignantly attacks a friend who had helped himself to one of Serapio's cigarettes.

Los ambiciosos (The Ambitious) treats the relationship between money and happiness. With the return of Rogelio to his old neighborhood after a year's absence in the wake of having won a fortune at the lottery and having lived elsewhere in luxury, we learn that he and his wife have lost their health, his daughter has been scorned, and his former happiness and peace of mind—formerly products of a simple life, hard work, and poverty—have now turned to "loneliness, sadness, boredom, and desperation."

These eleven playlets demonstrate the art of expounding a moral or social lesson without infusing the work unduly with thesis. Didactic considerations are skillfully tempered to be operative within the framework of the author's satirical pose. At no time does

Arniches' implicit position with regard to proper moral conduct loom larger than his explicit awareness that the true behavior of human beings will all too often unfold in that gray area between right and wrong, laughter and tears, love and hate.

Arniches was mistaken when he denied the artistic importance or literary transcendence of these sketches.[11] They are, because of their brevity and concision, veritable gems of dialectal literature, combining in capsulated form the mastery of a dialogue proportioned to the situation, the sparkle of a biting wit, and the eloquence of the edifying precept that hard work and purposeful living will build the moral fiber of a people and a nation. Also attesting to the literary value of the "rapid sainetes" is Arniches' characterization of the small, beaten, lost souls of Madrid. A picaresque tone attends the dramatization of their comical self-delusions, of the ever-present fear of hunger, pain, and suffering.

All of the characters in these sainetes belong to the lower social classes. United by their common struggle for existence, they have been hardened by the harshness of life. According to Arniches, their struggles deserve the respect due to heroism. He incorporates into their expressions of cynicism and misery the redeeming force of good humor and raillery, thereby fashioning out of the diversity and complexity of the human personality an assembly of believable contemporary folk types, reminiscent of the marvelous characters depicted in the writings of Benito Pérez Galdós. Arniches never made a secret of his affinity for this stratum of humanity: "I love picturesque customs, the noble and strange psychology of these good and happy folk of Madrid's poor districts, with their lively ingenuity, their impulsive emotions, their wit, banter, and merriment."[12]

Arniches' depiction of folk types in *From the Soul of Madrid* is a far cry from the festive spirit of *Isidra's Saint.* He now sides with the antiheroes, the poor and the humble and the oppressed from among the underprivileged masses. His indulgence and sympathy for these creatures cease, however, at the point where his characters manifest a resigned passivity. Arniches is reformistic in his attitude concerning the dulling effects of inaction. He deplores any tendency toward fatalistic thinking and opposes the negative restraint that leads many of his countrymen into a state of abulia.

Some of his characters voice the belief that physical inertia and spiritual stagnation are the best antidotes for troubled times. Arniches then utilizes satire, irony, or caricature to ridicule this attitude, denouncing the thinking of those who would, as José Monleón observes, "impede the improvement of their social level and limit their contribution to social progress."[13] Monleón laments the fact that Arniches' reputation with regard to these and other serious writings rests too heavily on his comical inserts. He acknowledges the fact that many modern critics err in judging the playwright categorically as a festive writer; they support the oft-repeated notion that the "sparkling and fixed vision of individuals" found in *Isidra's Saint* and other early plays is a constant trait that is reiterated throughout all of the author's theater. In reality, the majority of Arniches' plays after 1913 serve to repudiate this commonly held view which Monleón so perceptively counters.

The non-Madrilenean reader may encounter some difficulty with the "rapid sainetes." They are characterized by an extensive use of plebeian speech. Spelling conforms to phonetic deviations and the vocabulary is replete with localistic slang. More than in any of his previous or later plays, Arniches employs syntactical distortions and colloquial expressions to heighten the humor of the repartee and, more importantly perhaps, to establish a sense of linguistic rapport with his Madrilenean audience, to awaken their concern and empathy, through the medium of everyday language, for the problems of "those shaggy, filthy, grotesque, hungry, abandoned ragamuffins" of their city.[14] Indeed, both by design and by execution, *From the Soul of Madrid* is genuine homespun protest literature. The deliberate caricaturing of native figures, complemented by a unique and very native colloquial jargon, brings close to home "all of the tragedy endured by the alluring and picturesque common folk of Madrid."[15] On several occasions Arniches pauses a moment to address himself directly to his public, pleading for the kind of understanding that will unite the hearts of people in the same way the vernacular binds their thoughts.

From the Soul of Madrid is a mature piece of writing generated specifically for the citizenry of that city. Its short morality plays combine a profound knowledge of the Spanish capital with satirical humor and a firm preceptive resolve. It signals the revival of the nationally popular theater of the paso and also of the entremés, whose main charm also rests in its wit and dialogue. Yet, as traditional as the form may be, the lively content of the "rapid sainetes" speaks of living issues in a modern dialect to a twentieth-century public. It is for this reason that Arniches relies on some of these sketches to provide for him the inspiration for later more extensive works. [16] The social and moral problems contained in this collection become in many instances the basis for dramatic conflict in his three-act comedies, tragicomedies, and grotesque tragedies, for here also the criticism ranges from comments on customs, and social conventions, to observations about politics and ideologies.

Even within the restricted framework of the *género chico,* which Arniches cultivated through 1936, one finds perpetuated this legacy of realism. In particular, the admirable one-act sainete entitled *Los milagros del jornal (Miracles from the Daily Wage),* first performed in 1924, is a work of piercing human content that has its roots in the moral climate of the playlets in *From the Soul of Madrid.*

IV Los milagros del jornal (Miracles from the Daily Wage)

The miseries of a rueful subsistence concern Arniches in this outstanding drama, the last sainete he ever wrote in one act. It is perhaps his greatest achievement as a *sainetero.*

The plot purveys the interaction between an impoverished couple, Neme and Sidoro. Fearful of incurring her husband's wrath for her failure to stretch out a scant budget to cover the week's expenses, Neme has pawned his only Sunday suit. Upon learning that Sidoro has been invited to a friend's wedding, she attempts to reclaim the clothes. She appeals for money to her neighbor, Polonia, but Polonia's resources are similar to her own. Earlier, her entreaty to Felipe, the old pawnbroker, had only served to fill her with pain and loathing, for in return for the release of the suit, Felipe had invited her to enjoy certain intimacies with him, which she in anger had refused. Convinced now that Sidoro will punish her physically and, in a wider context, apprehensive that the future can only bring greater sorrow and privations, Neme reaches a state of desperate anguish and even entertains the notion of suicide.

Sidoro enters, searches for his suit, and discovers what Neme has done. Only the intervention of Polonia prevents him from beating her with a stick. In the course of their heated confrontation, the source of Neme's greatest sense of despair is disclosed, that of not being able to exact from her husband's earnings the kind of material comforts that she sees their neighbors, Andrea and Celedonio, enjoying. Celedonio and Sidoro are both bricklayers, and each man brings home an equal amount of money:

NEME: I'm desperate and I can't perform miracles with a miserable wage.
SIDORO: Others earn the same and you ought to see how well they eat and
        dress.
NEME: Not on that wage.
SIDORO: Yes, ma'am.
NEME: No, sir.
SIDORO: Yes, my dear. And over there, right across the hall, right through
        that wall, you have the example to make you ashamed.
NEME: What example?
SIDORO: Andrea and Celedonio. What is Celedonio? Just a simple brick-
        layer, with eight miserable pesetas, and you should see the food
        she carries to him at work. Why, there are days when three tooth-
        picks aren't enough!

Sidoro's insults expand on this topic and Neme becomes progressively more distraught, refusing to believe that their material
inferiority to Andrea and Celedonio could be the mere result of her
inadequacy as a homemaker.

The argument is interrupted as Celedonio and his son call for
Sidoro. Disappointed at not finding him able to attend the wedding,
they go on alone. During their absence, Felipe the pawnbroker
makes what is apparently one of his many treks to visit Andrea in her
apartment flat. Celedonio returns home early, however, owing
to his son's unexpected illness during the wedding ceremony. He
surprises his unfaithful wife in readiness to entertain Felipe. The
revelation of her infidelity effaces the trust of an eight-year marriage
and his heart is broken. We last see him leaving Sidoro's home,
weeping bitterly and brandishing a straight-edge razor in search of
the frightened and fleeing Felipe.

A terse and eloquent final scene finds Sidoro kneeling tenderly
at Neme's feet. He calls her a saint, kisses her hand, and cries,
"Long live poverty!" Thus, in only ten short scenes, Arniches
achieves what less skillful playwrights would not have accomplished
in fewer than three complete acts. The economy of the effort is
noteworthy, for the sainete stands in form as an example of its
genre, and in content as a brilliant summation of Arniches' artistic
and preceptive talent. Unlike the brief dialogues that comprise
From the Soul of Madrid, the characters are here described exclusively by what they say and by what others say about them. They are
unmistakable human beings; their actions and words bespeak the
application of a moderate naturalistic stamp, infusing them with a

credibility not apparent in the earlier sainetes and zarzuelas. The value of this convincing characterization is the fact that it comes off with such ease within a remarkably concentrated framework of half an hour's time of actual staging. Had Arniches continued to write in this vein rather than expand his sainetes into lengthy comedies, his reputation would have been enhanced a hundred-fold.[17]

Miracles from the Daily Wage has provoked several interesting comments on the subject of the author's purpose in presenting an abbreviated case history of severe economic privation. Following the play's première, Spanish critics were startled by the ticklish implications in its treatment and by what was still for them a novel direction for Arniches to follow. In some reviews it was labeled a dangerous piece and its author a revolutionist.[18] Others, stressing the positive moral lesson of the play, which extols honor and sacrifice over immoral surrender, considered the work a proclamation of "the triumph of the spirit."[19]

José Monleón, on the other hand, sees in its writing an example of Arniches' apparent belief that "the knavery of the underprivileged is a consequence of the shameless conduct of the upper classes."[20] By this token, Andrea's acts of prostitution are more to be pitied than censured, for she, like the luckless petty thief in the aforenamed *The Scientific Couple,* is obliged to sin due to the indifference of a society that refuses to examine itself critically and to undertake a collective improvement. This position seems more in line with the recent efforts to vindicate Arniches as a serious reformist writer.[21]

Belonging as it does to Arniches' period of prime creations, succeeding such highly-regarded plays as *Los caciques (The Bosses),* and three of his grotesque tragedies, it is no wonder that *Miracles from the Daily Wage* was a great success. Since the publication of his "rapid sainetes" to this final effort in the *género chico,* Arniches had written thirty-four plays, only eleven of which were works of collaboration. The majority of his writings of unaided composition were longer than one act. In other words, by this date—1924— Arniches was no longer entrenched in the then decadent age of the *género chico;* at the age of fifty-eight he had become converted to productions of greater length and greater complexity. From this time until his death nineteen years later, he would be recognized as a writer dedicated to the so-called *género grande.*

CHAPTER 5

The Voice of Conscience: Three Major Works of Protest

UNDERLYING the action of his more than 190 plays, Arniches often develops an explicit exemplary thesis. "My ideal," he once wrote to the literary historian, Julio Cejador y Frauca, "is a simple and humble one. It corresponds to the modesty of my literary rank. With my sainetes and farces I aspire solely to stimulate the noble temper of the people and to help them see the vileness of evil instincts."[1] This preceptive intent has prompted some writers to consider Arniches a playwright who successfully approximates the critical posture of the Generation of '98, as was pointed out in an earlier chapter. Arniches, however, tends to subordinate his pronouncements of moral truth to the more frequent humorous depictions of human conflict, interwoven with realistic and picturesque sketches of *costumbrismo*. A lesson of kind guiding wisdom is constantly imbedded in the action, but carefully held in check so as to lend emphasis and credence to the plot line. In several of his didactic writings an evil trait, such as envy, avarice, or incontinence, gives rise to serious complications which, in the course of time, resolve themselves in such a way that the evil is exposed and goodness reaffirmed. The playwright can thus convey the object lesson of his play without too much moralistic rhetoric.

Such is the case with the three-act melodrama, *Rositas de olor (Fragrant Little Roses)*, wherein the heartache of a poor orphan girl stems from the greed of other men. The process by which the heroine changes adversity into happiness carries sufficient didactic force and requires no overt pronouncements to condemn the villainy of covetousness. Other examples among many include *La divisa (The Emblem)*, in which Arniches launches an attack on envy by describing its effect on the attitudes and actions of his characters; and the doleful sainete *La pena negra (The Dark Affliction)*, in which the author reminds his audience that life offers much sorrow and bitterness despite love's dominion over all opposing forces.

These early plays are representative of a didactic tendency that broadens in poignancy and wields an incisive edge in later writings.

With the staging of *Miss Trevélez* in 1916, Arniches brings his preceptive bias to an artistic culmination. From this date on the author's plays tend to promote a thesis made crystal-clear by overt statement rather than by mere implication. This is especially apparent in the serialized "rapid sainetes" which we have discussed. Irritated by his countrymen's adherence to the rigid norms of a fossilized, monotonous existence, Arniches now speaks out with a dynamic voice of protest. Avoiding the pessimistic tone so characteristic of many prominent writers of the period, and eschewing as well any hint of resignation in the face of the disappointing social, moral, and political trends of his day, the aging playwright, now over fifty years old, endeavors to awaken his compatriots to a sense of shame for their dishonesty *(The Bosses),* their bigotry *(The Heroic Town),* and their idleness *(Miss Trevélez).* He seeks, moreover, to encourage his audience to face the future with new courage and constructive thinking. Denouncing evil with the tools of humor, satire, and irony, Arniches employs his dramatic talents to help reform the nation.

I *Political Criticism:* Los caciques (The Bosses)

Administrative corruption in rural Spain is the theme of *The Bosses,* a patriotic denunciation of political tyranny. The play takes place in a sad and forgotten provincial town where "everything is old, furtive, without a sense of reform." For Arniches the unnamed town is symbolic of national despoliation, out of which has sprung the origin of the decadence of Spain.

The first act defines the infamous rule of Don Acisclo, who for eighteen years has wielded a despotic control over the lives, finances, and morale of his townspeople. Three citizens attempt to register their respective complaints, only to be vilified by Acisclo. The mayor's reign of terror seems assured of continuation until a letter comes announcing the imminent arrival of a delegate from Madrid, who has been sent to investigate charges of extortion and ruthlessness. Pepe Ojeda and his nephew Alfredo, two poor travelers in search of their former lovers, are mistaken for the official representative and his secretary. They are astounded to find themselves greeted by an exhibition of fanfare and flattery, designed to dissuade them from condemning the town's deceitful officials.

The humor of the second act ensues from the willingness of Pepe and Alfredo to accept the mayor's overwhelming display of generosity, consisting of fine food, comfortable lodging, gifts, money, and the presence of two young ladies who happen to be their former sweethearts. Don Acisclo is intent on blinding them with bribery, hopeful they will overlook his dishonest record. Only in the closing scene of this act do Pepe and Alfredo realize that the acclamation is a sham resulting from the mayor's fear and cowardice, and that the honors they have received do in truth disguise a deep sense of contempt on the town's part toward any threat to reform municipal corruption.

Aware of the physical danger to which they are now exposed, Pepe and Alfredo ready their escape in the third act, enlisting the aid of a handful of trusted townsfolk who have suffered the most from the mayor's intimidations. With the sudden, unannounced arrival of the real delegate from Madrid, the deception is revealed and Don Acisclo's tyranny comes to an end.

The plot of *The Bosses* is clearly patterned after Nikolai Gogol's five-act comedy of 1836, *The Inspector General.* The situations are very similar and the barbed satire is identical, although Arniches tends to sacrifice character depth for thesis, whereas Gogol places greater emphasis on the development of Ivan Khlestakov, the vagabond mistaken for a high official, and on the imperious personality of Anton Antonovich, the town mayor. Inspired as he may well have been by Gogol's play, Arniches' primary intent is more didactic than dramatic, and all too often his oratory weakens the continuity of the action.

The characterization in *The Bosses* is deliberately slighted to give priority to an expansion of the author's basic premise: "The Spanish people will not be able to shout with joy, 'Long live Spain!' until we have eradicated once and for all the threat of bossism." Some critics have called attention to the fact that Arniches' generic villains and heroes resemble the conceptual puppets of Jacinto Benavente's masterpiece, *Los intereses creados (The Bonds of Interest).*[2] The comparison is apt insofar as Arniches profits from the Benaventine model of dramatizing representative symbols as the incarnation of the evil interests which debilitate the values of a sound society.

Arniches' point of view is strictly political, however. His characters confine their activity to a local municipal sphere, shorn of the complex social dimensions to be found in Benavente's work. Arniches formulates his feelings about conditions in his country by manipulating the words and actions of his marionette figures to attack the same tender questions that preoccupied Alfonso XIII in his endeavor to combat the political bosses of Spain.[3]

The Bosses is a work of energetic criticism. Its value resides in the author's didactic insistence that Christian virtues represent valid precepts for political dealings. This is Arniches' first and most significant play about political morality.[4] In a later play, *El padre Pitillo (Father Pitillo)*, he dramatizes a similar conflict, pitting justice against the power of money and high station. Here too the political leaders do not feel bound by common law to uphold the dignity and noble principles of their office. At no time in his political expressions does Arniches embrace a party line or endorse a specific ideological issue. He addresses himself to social-political problems, but resists being classified with the social theater of his day by virtue of the constructive moral intention he pursues in his plays, as contrasted with the striking ideological posture which prompted such writings as *Juan José* (1895) and *El señor feudal (The Feudal Lord)* (1897) by his boyhood friend, Joaquín Dicenta.

Nor does Arniches advocate political reform, uprisings, unionizing, revolutions, demonstrations, or strikes. His is a "happy obsession with goodness," to cite the words of Juan Emilio Aragonés.[5] This is to say, it is the playwright's contention that social and political problems are best resolved by an untiring devotion to the high moral principles of honesty and integrity. He remains committed to the notion that mutual understanding and love are the best tools for building the fabric of social and political order. Ironically, though, Arniches' benevolence has endeared him so to his public that the social impact of his most sincere and fervent protests—*The Bosses* is the best example—has more often than not been diluted. Many devoted playgoers have esteemed such "serious" plays to be a regrettable departure from the carefree formulas of debonair *costumbrismo*.

II *Social Criticism:* La heroica villa (The Heroic Town)

Embedding caustic social criticism within three acts of entertaining humor, Arniches reveals the hypocrisy and the spiritual petrifaction of Villanea, a fictitious Castilian town.

The arrival of Isabel de Reinosa, a wealthy, widowed baroness from Madrid, gives rise to much public flurry in Villanea. In the first act the townsfolk are characterized through their response to the elegant aristocrat's coming. The men, for the most part, are possessed by voluptuous yearning for the visitor. The town's gallants wager as to who will first seduce Isabel. Young husbands stare at her longingly; old men dream about her wistfully. The women of Villanea, envious of her beauty and refinement, feel threatened by her intrusion. They ostracize her from their social functions and greet her with insults.

One of the main figures to foment hatred toward Isabel is the town priest, Father Lacorza, who cannot detach himself from traditional ideas and sees sin in the least deviation from old customs. His antagonist is Isabel's kindly protector, Don Fabio, an upholder of the constructive human and social values found wanting in the townspeople. When Isabel engages a young disillusioned artist to complete his unfinished portrait of her, the women of the town are aroused to full fury. They accuse the baroness of immoral motives and vow to drive her out of Villanea.

Act Two dwells at length on the prudery and intolerance of the women of Villanea. They concoct fantastic charges with which to slander Isabel's reputation. The baroness attempts to ignore their calumnies. A symbol of Christian charity and nobility, she proceeds to found a hospital in Villanea and plans other humanitarian acts for the town's underprivileged citizens. She discourages all amorous advances from the lustful men and tries to pacify their wives' wrath with her accustomed courtesy. But all to no avail. Continued attacks on her character from the pulpit incite the women to even greater hostility, and the second act closes with a strong foreboding of calamity.

The third act opens with Isabel's return to Villanea following a week's absence, only to discover that the windows of her home are shattered, the telephone lines are cut, and the water conduit is broken. Fearing a malicious attack on her person, she sends for Don Fabio, who arrives in time to prevent a mob of angry women from injuring or murdering the baroness. While Don Fabio recriminates the throng of furies for their blind and irrational rage, Isabel quietly drives away, abandoning the "heroic" town of Villanea forever.

The author's moral lesson is made explicit through Don Fabio's impassioned address to the intolerant women of Villanea:

As is the case with many women in many Spanish towns, instead of educating your spirit by way of culture and tolerance, you have imprisoned yourselves in old prejudices, you have invented false moral values, and you still believe that any woman who cares for her person with exquisite care and attempts to beautify herself in order to magnify her charms can be neither decent nor virtuous. . . Elegance is not an improvised thing, it is an education. It is not a color nor a fashion; it is kindness and delicacy. It is a finely cultivated product that you carry in your soul. . .

Isabel's final departure from Villanea signifies the withdrawal of the spirit of human understanding from a state of rigid provincial-mindedness. Carlos Arniches once again demonstrates through the use of symbolic characters that the social milieu is deprived of excellence when fanaticism and prudishness are allowed to reign.

The play borders on the grotesque insofar as the townspeople are portrayed with strokes of caricature to make their exaggerated traits appear ridiculous. Comedy lightens the caustic bite of the satire and, as is Arniches' custom, the villains are depicted as laughable, silly figures. Their weaknesses are rendered on a social rather than personal level, for Arniches aims his volleys constructively at a universal failing instead of censuring the individual. Whereas in some of his other plays of social intent he attacks the aristocracy and its reactionary mentality, such as in *La casa de Quirós (The Quirós Manor)* and *Vivir de ilusiones (Living on Dreams)*, he here levels his criticism at the lower- to middle-class evils, concluding that Spain's social problems would be greatly reduced were the vices of intolerance and insensibility converted into hard work and forbearance. The play's ironic title alone suggests that the heroism of Old Castile has been degraded by an unchanging preservation of old beliefs, beliefs fostered by ignorance, prejudice, and lack of charity toward one's fellowmen.

III *Moral Criticism:* La Señorita de Trevélez (Miss Trevélez)

Literary historians and drama critics generally agree that this three-act tragic farce "marks the point of Arniches' artistic maturity and realism."[6] It represents "one of the most important theatrical works of Spanish contemporary dramatic art."[7]

The first act takes place in the reading room of a social club in an indeterminate "third-rate provincial capital" of Spain. A sense of static monotony prevails. Tedium, inertia, human lassitude—the debilitating ingredients which for Arniches are the chief products of the collective indolence of a small town—have combined with the petty jealousy of one insensitive young man to occasion the fabrication of a vicious prank. Pablo Picavea, vying for the attentions of the Trevélez' servant Solita, has hatched a vengeful practical joke for his rival, the kindly Numeriano Galán, by conspiring to forge a marriage proposal in Galán's handwriting, directed to Florita Trevélez, a naive, ugly, romantic, middle-aged spinster. The primary intent of this letter is to undermine Galán's amorous prospects. A secondary aim is to ridicule both Florita and Galán for the sake of a good laugh.

Florita lives in an unreal world of dream-built sentimentality. Her illusory existence is fashioned on the one hand by her uncritical absorption of mawkish movie plots, and on the other by the over-protective adoration of her brother, Don Gonzalo, who is totally devoted to the mission of reinforcing her state of happiness and ease by appearing young, by dressing with flamboyance, and by speaking in a flowery manner unsuitable to his fifty years. When Don Gonzalo learns of Galán's proposal he is ecstatic, and bends all efforts to support and to expedite his long-desired dream of marrying Flora to a deserving man. Galán, for his part, is helplessly enmeshed in the cruel joke, unable to confess the truth for fear of incurring Don Gonzalo's reputed wrath. He is also overcome by the widespread public acclamation which his engagement to Flora has produced.

The second act begins two weeks later in the Trevélez garden, amidst the lights and color and gaiety of an evening party that Don Gonzalo has arranged in honor of the betrothed couple. Galán by now is desperate to find an escape. The joke has reached unbearable proportions, and his agitation is constantly aggravated by Don Gonzalo's impassioned rhetoric and by Florita's chatter about romance and bliss. The pranksters, concerned about Galán's unstable state of mind, attempt to extricate him from the dilemma by concocting a new scheme. They endeavor to bring Picavea face to face with Florita as another pretender for her hand. His major role is to vilify Galán in the girl's eyes. The plan then calls for a confrontation and a resultant duel between the two rivals, thus affording Galán a chance to renounce his engagement, either by a feigned injury or by a retreat in the name of personal honor.

The plot is only halfway successful. Don Gonzalo intervenes while Picavea is defaming Galán's character. He challenges the rascal to a legitimate duel. Galán is thus reinstated with greater backing as Flora's worthy suitor, and he now seems destined to become her husband as a result of the infamous farce.

In Act Three Don Gonzalo is priming himself for his fencing duel with Picavea, but the physical encounter never materializes. First Galán, then Picavea himself, come to visit Don Gonzalo in his gymnasium. They disclose to him the details of the original practical joke and its perverse ramifications. The degrading nature and consequences of the prank are discussed, leaving all parties humbled and ashamed. As the play ends, Don Gonzalo is left with the thankless task of breaking the news to his cherished sister.

According to Pérez de Ayala, *Miss Trevélez* is, in its substance and purpose, "one of the most serious, most human, and most captivating plays" of its time, a drama that "while provoking laughter with frequency, is a deeply sad work."[8] These attributes spring from the pathetic and convincing thesis set forth within Arniches' accustomed framework of genial humor. Indeed, notwithstanding the clever wit in dialogue and in situation, the penetrating moral seriousness of the play is so clearly emphasized that Arniches comes very close to overstressing his position. He extends the full particulars of the cruel prank over all three acts, then devotes much of the conversation of the final scenes to a discursive reaffirmation of the pernicious repercussions underlying the misuse of idleness. To this end, had Carlos Arniches written nothing but this outstanding didactic play, his name would be identified more among those who adamantly denounced the social and moral ills besetting Spain in the socio-aesthetic movement of 1898, than as one whose cheerful *costumbrismo* usually relegates him to the subcategory of a comic entertainer. Arniches' proposed corrective for the malady of cruelty fostered by indolence is stated in the final scene: "The way to get rid of this nationally-typed company of scoffers is to disseminate culture. We must kill them with books; there is no other way. Culture tempers sensibility, and when these youngsters become educated, they will no longer be capable of such evil, they will no longer dare to shatter a heart in jest, nor embitter a life with a practical joke."

The premium that Arniches places on education as a redemptive tool to elevate the moral and intellectual tone of the social order is one in spirit with the efforts of such idealistic thinkers as Joaquín Costa (1844–1911) and Francisco Giner de los Ríos (1839–1915), whose liberal and renovative teachings gave origin and impetus to the first independent educative center in Spain. Arniches' idealism is likewise closely allied to that of the novelist Benito Pérez Galdós (1843–1920), whose sympathetic regard for even the worst of his creations had no small impact on the nature of the former's dramatic humor. Arniches thus belongs to that fraternity of constructive humanists who with their pens exalted the virtue of hard work, love, tolerance, sacrifice, and perseverance as remedies to combat the degenerative forces at work on the national scene and in the national character.

Aside from its exemplary tendency, *Miss Trevélez* is a notable artistic achievement. A gradual shift from the comic domain of illusion into the tragic sphere of reality gives depth to the bittersweet farce that implicates all of the characters. Florita appears only on the margin of the main action; as the innocent and unsuspecting victim of the hoax, she is tragic only by implication, while her actual stage appearance elicits laughter due to the timeless world in which she gyrates as an unconsciously ridiculous figure. Her attitudes, actions, and language bespeak a woman quite removed from reality; hence, despite having her name featured in the play's title, her role is incidental to the vital unfolding of the tragedy.

Numeriano Galán is similarly stereotyped as a pathetic creature. His lack of courage to uncover the hoax makes his anguish appear funny. Attempting to reach the rapturous heights of Florita's dreamworld, so not to reveal to her his true antipathy for her, Galán only plunges more deeply into the agony of his own foolish reality. His is a comic debate between a longing to escape and a goading sense of integrity urging him to disembarrass himself honorably from the deception. Whereas Flora is a living parody of romantic otherworldliness, Galán is frozen as a laughable symbol of paralysis due to his fear of Don Gonzalo and to his own inherent cowardliness.

The truly tragic figure is Don Gonzalo. Unlike Florita, he is conscious of the ridiculous impression he exhibits. Striving to camouflage his age, Don Gonzalo deliberately sacrifices his own happiness in order to conceal the pain of time's passing from his spinster sister, and thus prevent her world of imagination from crumbling away. A man of noble fiber and absurd behavior, he appears as both clown and hero. His complicated personality pervades the chiaroscuro between farcical caricature and tragic realism. Enraptured over the news of Galán's proposal, he falls so completely into the fanciful realm of his sister's aspiration that he risks the loss of his authentic bearing and allows his abandonment to illusion to preclude Galán's chances of clarifying the hoax any sooner. Conversely, when told of the deception, tragic reality becomes his most intimate possession; now the grotesque distortions of his previous conduct and language are replaced by an heroic acceptance of the truth, articulated in clear, unaffected terms. It is this ultimate act of heroism which saves Don Gonzalo from deteriorating in the face of the lie he has lived and the grief of having been victimized by an act of treachery.

Don Gonzalo is a caricatured tragic hero. His initial character flaw, exaggerated for comic effect, is his overeagerness for great expectations. This weakness leads him from innocence through self-deception to self-realization, the same evolution through which many of Arniches' protagonists pass in their quest for moral strength. Within a framework of comedy, Don Gonzalo's serious dimension makes him a prototype of the grotesque hero, that is, the laughable, pitiable, and pathetic character who is at one and the same time a tragic and comic figure. As one of Arniches' strongest creations, Don Gonzalo foretokens the portrayal of Don Antonio in the distinguished grotesque tragedy, *Es mi hombre (That's My Man)*.

CHAPTER 6

The Grotesque Tragedies

A RNICHES was over fifty when he wrote the first play that he captioned with the singular title of grotesque tragedy. He was then two thirds of the way into his career and brought to this new and curious class of drama a competence gleaned from his fascination for the theater and nourished by his infatuation for the magic of the human personality. He wrote six grotesque tragedies, though a number of his other plays, such as *Miss Trevélez,* contain elements not unlike those which distinguish the grotesque tragedy from writings of other dramatic formulas.

I *A General Concept of the Grotesque Tragedy*

The concept of the grotesque as Arniches applied the term to his own dimension of dramatic expression has been broadly and somewhat vaguely defined since Ramón Pérez de Ayala first acknowledged with sharp clarity the greatness of the new form following the appearance of *Miss Trevélez* and *¡Que viene mi marido! (My Husband's Coming!).* For Ayala the grotesque tragedy is an exaggeration of comedy, an insistence on the impact of farce for the sake of caricaturization; or, as Pérez de Ayala also indicated, it is tragedy in reverse; that is, a tragedy in which the protagonist does not die, but must survive to face whatever crisis may befall him.[1]

Teodoro Lipps, writing some four years after Ayala's essays first appeared, attempted to summarize the meaning of the grotesque tragedy as being "that class of comedy which offers us caricature, exaggeration, contortion, the incredible, the monstrous, the fantastic, all employed to produce a comic effect."[2]

A decade later, Melchor Fernández Almagro brought this notion into relation with Arniches' philosophical attitude toward those creatures for whom the playwright felt a deep compassion and devotion: the citizens of Madrid. Viewing the grotesque tragedy as a modern concept of the world and of life, Fernández Almagro states that as a new form of art, it affords us "a glimpse at the world of one's deepest feelings through the keyhole of ingenuousness."[3]

More recent critics, such as Pedro Salinas, have concentrated their remarks on the transformation of the hero of the grotesque tragedy. For Salinas, Arniches achieves his sense of the grotesque by imposing upon the hero a series of peculiar circumstances which change his outward show of comedy into a perfectly serious situation.[4] According to Vicente Ramos, such a transformation is the logical outgrowth of Arniches' profound understanding of people and is operative through the author's eagerness to state a moral principle entrenched in realism and the human condition.[5] The grotesque tragedy, affirms Ramos, is an aesthetic consequence of the sainete, having evolved in a natural way from Arniches' earlier writings.

A review of the several plots and properties of a number of grotesque tragedies will serve better to enhance our understanding of this unique genre than the further accumulation of general definitions and interpretations. Following our examination of Arniches' most estimable plays, it will prove helpful to formulate a list of characteristics which, by and large, are applicable to the several grotesque tragedies that he wrote between 1918 and 1933.

II ¡Que viene mi marido! (My Husband's Coming!)

Combining an improbable plot with humorous, fast action, *My Husband's Coming!* is, by its very resistance to verisimilitude, a noteworthy example of the grotesque tragedy.

The first act discloses the fact that Carita, the daughter of middle-class parents from Madrid, will inherit an immense fortune from her godfather provided she be widowed. Luis, the girl's fiancé, is deeply troubled, as are her mother and two uncles, over this bizarre arrangement. They unitedly accept the suggestion from one of Luis' friend that Carita marry a doomed hospital patient, upon whose death she can legally claim the inheritance. Carita requires much persuasion but finally agrees to the plan. The marriage *in articulo mortis* takes place immediately.

In Act Two Bermejo, the "dying" husband, is still very much alive. Pleading chronic poverty in the last days of his mortal existence, he installs himself in the home of his new in-laws and leads a luxurious life at their expense. With picaresque cunning, Bermejo extorts great sums of money while apparently yearning for death. The family is willing to indulge the dying Bermejo, but all efforts to hasten his demise end in frustration. As Act Two closes, Bermejo leaps out of the balcony window in a desperate suicide attempt, only to land uninjured on the awning below. He reenters the house lamenting his complete indestructibility.

Further extortion brings Bermejo's now despairing hosts to the brink of bankruptcy in the final act. The situation seems hopeless when suddenly an old friend of Bermejo's appears. The visitor introduces himself as Saturnino, a partner in crime with the scoundrel Menacho, who is the same man posing as Bermejo. The real Bermejo had died in the hospital as anticipated. Saturnino, the brother of the deceased patient, had been promised but not paid a share of the profits from Menacho's attempted blackmail scheme. Carita is, after all, the legal widow of Bermejo and can now inherit her fortune and marry Luis. The family is overjoyed and the two rogues are rudely dismissed. The play ends with a customary moral pronouncement: "This was punishment for your greed. That which I told you before is most certainly the truth: that a man's pocket resembles his stomach. If you desire good health, you must eat well; if you desire happiness, you must obtain money through honest means."

Critical judgment of this grotesque tragedy has ranged from Eduardo M. del Portillo's disparaging remark that it represents one of Arniches' worst plays, to Pérez de Ayala's flattering endorsement of the work as an authentic expression of the characteristic Spanish trait of insensibility.[6]

The play follows its own laws of causality, a fact which would tend to disturb anyone prone to evaluate it by the norms of verisimilitude. It is this element of improbability, however, which accounts largely for the play's charm and humor. The events surrounding Menacho's artful designs on his victims' money while pretending to be Bermejo, and the family's increasing agitation to expedite his death constitute the play's focal interest. Seizing the multiple possibilities for comic effect inherent in this plot line, Arniches develops the personality of Bermejo-Menacho with a touch of caricature. He portrays a type whose exaggerated rascality reminds us of the very human and much-to-be-pitied *frescos* in the one-act farces that Arniches wrote with García Álvarez, while exhibiting at the same time infamous cunning of the classical *pícaro,* an antihero driven by hunger, exuberant through deceit, and ultimately exposed for overindulging in his craft. When Menacho oversteps the bounds of discreet villainy, his cocky self-assurance reaches the point of self-caricature, and in the end his dialogue and deliberations bespeak a pathetic, unheroic little man. He succumbs not to death or dishonor in the tragic manner; he must simply return again to face the world with his old stratagems. In his parting words to the family, he declares that much of his villainy was merely a sham and that, as we observed in our discussion about the thief in the rapid sainete, *The Scientific Couple,* his exploits were the outgrowth of personal privation and society's distrust: "Thank you, ladies and gentlemen," he says sincerely, "I have appeared to be more treacherous than I really am. Need, hunger. . . . Forgive me!"

The protagonist Menacho and his betrayer Saturnino stand out in bold relief as the only characters in the play from the lower stratum of society. These are the types with which Arniches is most effective in his character delineations. These are the figures he knows best, having plumbed the moral, intellectual, and spiritual fiber of their being in many previous writings. The other characters of the play belong to middle-class Madrilenean society and are individualized with less authenticity; their actions are not as convincing as those of the underworld scoundrels. Each is portrayed with the indulgent satire of an author who frowns charitably on their materialistic aims, and seeks to draw a moral lesson from their insensitivity to hard work and sound honesty.

III Es mi hombre (That's My Man)

Chronologically the second of his grotesque tragedies, this is Arniches' best play of the genre and stands as one of his all-time masterworks. It offers one of the best examples in his repertory of the marriage of humor with pathos.

The first act finds Don Antonio, a timid, pusillanimous, but good-hearted man of fifty, living in wretched poverty with his seventeen-year-old daughter, Leonor. Antonio has been unemployed for four months and faces an impending eviction from the shabby apartment unless he can find work. In desperation he has accepted an ignominious job as a walking advertisement, for which he must wear a ridiculous large-headed mask. His daughter is horrified at the grotesque figure he exhibits and forbids him to accept such humiliation.

When all of their efforts to overcome poverty suggest the inevitability of utter destitution, Antonio is offered a good-paying

position as a bouncer and inspector at the Andorra House, a local
gambling casino. The nature of the work is completely foreign to
Antonio's cowardly disposition and small stature, but the realization
that his daughter is suffering with cold and hunger imbues him with
the assurance that he will somehow find sufficient stamina to discharge his duties. As the first act closes, the grotesque situation has
been clearly defined: Antonio, a weak, indecisive, and frightened
little man, must now simulate the role of a brave and fearless
bouncer, and risk, as his daughter fears, serious injury or certain
death at the hands of savage ruffians.

As Act Two opens, Antonio has been employed by the casino
for four days and has in that time cleared it of all troublemakers.
His success is attributed to his having assumed an air of cold indifference before the threats of local toughs, and thus far, to his own
astonishment, his feigned callousness has earned him the reputation
of a tyrant. Internally, however, Antonio remains a terrified weak-
ling. In his moments of nervous strain and fear, he turns first to
drink then to the irresistible charms of Sole, a barroom woman of
easy virtue who plans to divest him of his earnings.

This plunge into misery and shame is momentarily put aside
when Antonio is informed that three ruthless bandits have declared
their intention of killing him. Convinced that he must flee to save
his life, he is about to escape when the ruffians arrive. Leonor,
entering the casino at the same time in search of her father, is
suddenly accosted by the bullies and made to suffer indignities at
their hands. Her father, seeing that the girl's honor is at stake, now
finds true courage to fight the three bandits, who flee in haste for
their lives. The feat solidifies Antonio's reputation as a man of great
daring, and as a reward for his valor he receives ten thousand
pesetas. Wealthy and elated, Antonio now shifts his attentions back
again to the ever-present seductress, Sole.

In Act Three Leonor and her boyfriend, Marcos, are distressed
to find Antonio in a state of total dissipation. He has squandered
his money on Sole and has sought comfort from his anxieties in
alcohol. Leonor determines to find work and thereby keep her
father from returning to the casino. She charges her fiancé with the
task of throwing Sole out of her father's home, but Marcos likewise
falls victim to Sole's allurements. It now becomes Leonor's duty
to assert herself; she banishes the evil woman and restores her
father to a sense of dignity.

In the play's final scenes the most dangerous threat to Antonio's cowardly nature appears in the person of Quemarropa, a notorious bully from Seville. Quemarropa has come to Antonio's home to challenge his bravery. At Leonor's request, Antonio and Marcos engage in a mock struggle in the back room, thus disarming Quemarropa's self-assurance and causing him to flee in terror. The play ends as Antonio agrees to renounce his make-believe calling in order to live in the quiet serenity of the protection of Marcos and Leonor, who announce their intent to combine their modest salaries for a blissful marriage.

The two principal characters emerge on separate planes of heroism. Leonor's role is clear and uncomplicated: she embodies the ideal modern Spanish girl whose usefulness to others increases as she expands her independence and initiative. As is the case with most of Arniches' heroines, Leonor is a dominant force for good, exercising common sense and ingenuity to promote virtue in her milieu. Antonio is the more interesting in that he is a perfect example of nothing in particular. He manifests the pathetic predicament of a sad little man who yearns to free himself from reversals in the face of his own inadequacy to overcome them. He is the typical "pitiful fellow" or "sad soul" *(pobre hombre)* depicted by Arniches in several plays, beginning with the timid but noble figure of Venancio in *Isidra's Saint* and repeated in a score of later tragicomic works in which the protagonists' sufferings are overplayed to give emphasis to their comical self-delusions.

Antonio's finest hour comes in the unforgettable twelfth scene of the second act, wherein his paternal love becomes an imperative for duty and his inherent timidity gives way to true courage. His strength is extracted from the sorry design of his weakness, providing the spectator with a moral philosophy couched in paradox. Antonio articulates the play's lesson in his closing words from the third act: "When men have to save their lives and the honor of their loved ones, all are courageous, because courage is the fulfillment of duty."

The theme of a coward disguised by bravado does not by itself produce the sense of tension and disfiguration germane to the notion of a grotesque tragedy. Arniches achieves the kind of over-tragic effect associated with the humor of this quasi-serious genre by contrasting and juxtaposing grimness of situation with levity of dialogue. The author's sustained compassion for the weakness of his characters prevents any hint of sarcasm, and the irony so prevalent in the mordant social criticism of *Miss Trevélez* is also conspicuously absent in *That's My Man,* although a social commentary is made manifest in the representation of the old Spanish aristocrat, Don Antonio, who, having lost his former wealth and position, must accept employment beneath his social station in order to survive. That which does stand out in *That's My Man* is Arniches' remarkable fusion of human affliction with comic relief, the mixture of pain and laughter.

Initially the spectator is distressed over the extreme indigence of Antonio and his daughter. The pathos born of their discomfiture intensifies as the threat of hunger—a leitmotif which accompanies the protagonist much in the same way that hunger stalks the *picaro*—torments Antonio and constrains him to accept an undignified job as a walking advertisement. The gravity of the situation argues for a serious and solemn dialogue, but quite the reverse occurs. Arniches superimposes upon the action a lighthearted tone which ensues from comments that Antonio makes about his miserable plight, comments which conceal the hero's internal anguish in much the same way that the grotesque mask he must wear as a walking advertisement hides his humiliation, and the air of valor he must assume as a casino bouncer is a masquerade for his fears. External humor thus obliges the spectator to forget momentarily the hunger and misery that Leonor and her father are suffering. Yet our recognition of Antonio's pathetic loss of contact with the authentic reality of his own being, a thesis reinforced by repeated caricature and by the fact that Antonio is himself aware of his ridiculous state, deepens our sense of compassion for his inward heartache. Explaining his ordeal to his unsympathetic landlord, Antonio says: "I am a poor fellow, defeated and frightened by penury, and because I have a child and wish to struggle to save her from this shipwreck of my life; for if it were not for her, I would already have left this place, and rather than have become a common bum, I would have placed myself where men are found who have a sense of dignity when they are unjustly mistreated."

As a final observation regarding *That's My Man,* it should be pointed out in Arniches' defense that the play is not a carbon copy of Leonid Andreyev's tragicomedy, *He Who Gets Slapped,* as Melchor Fernández Almagro has erroneously maintained.[7] In Andreyev's play, first premièred four years before *That's My Man,* the father, Count Mancini, is a heartless egomaniac whose only concern for Consuelo, his daughter, is to marry her to the highest bidder. The Count's only resemblance to Don Antonio is the fact that he too is an impoverished nobleman who is forced to live on his only child's earnings. The daughter in this case is a bareback rider in a circus. She is ultimately murdered, and her killer, disguised as a clown, commits suicide. Andreyev's play ends tragically, quite unlike any of the benign grotesque tragedies of Carlos Arniches. Any similarity between the two plays is too minimal to argue convincingly for a case of direct literary influence.

IV La locura de Don Juan (Don Juan's Madness)

Following the success of *That's My Man,* Arniches faced the difficult challenge of writing a play that would measure up to the public and critical acclaim accorded his appealing masterpiece. His third grotesque tragedy, staged sixteen months later, may indeed have fallen short of the mark, as his critics were quick to observe, being perhaps too close in spirit and subject matter to the former production, but in its dramatic structure, *Don Juan's Madness* is one of Carlos Arniches' strongest plays.

The action takes place in the Madrid home of a weak-willed, gentle and cowardly man named Don Juan, whose luxury-prone and despotic wife and daughter and two parasitic in-laws are ruining him financially and treating him with disrespect. He has lost their esteem by indulging their status-seeking whims and by failing to discharge his own domestic and financial duties with determination. As a result of his chronic lack of stamina and a nagging despair over his impending bankruptcy, Juan suffers from severe headaches. His physician, realizing that a decisive psychological treatment is essential, devises a therapeutic scheme that will restore Juan to his position as the authoritative head of the house. He convinces Juan that by swallowing a mysterious pill, a complete transformation will take place in his character; he will acquire an unassailable moral strength which will oblige others to obey his will.

While Juan is resting, the physician calls the family together to explain that Don Juan's headaches indicate that the man is on the verge of a dangerous type of insanity. The doctor cautions them not to counter his wishes in any way, for Juan, if driven to an attack of madness, is capable of an act of violence, including murder. As the first act draws to a close, Juan's reentrance causes utter chaos. In answer to an impulse to go hunting, he has procured his shotgun. The gun has a shell lodged in its barrel and accidentally fires, killing the parrot. The entire household, believing that Juan has suffered the attack of madness predicted by the doctor, is thrown completely awry.

As the second act opens, Juan has assumed complete command of all domestic and financial considerations. However, the power he wields is the result of fear, not affection. His physician now feels obliged to confess to Juan the truth about the deception, but he urges him to continue the pretense until Juan's financial crisis has passed. Juan undertakes some important adjustments, such as discharging several servants and ousting his in-laws. As a consequence of his mastery, Juan conquers the heretofore imperious wills of his wife and daughter, and intimidates with benevolence those who would otherwise have taken advantage of him.

In Act Three Juan is finally overcome by a sense of despair. He realizes that his false insanity has only alienated his loved ones. He discloses the sham, to which his wife and daughter respond with indignation by announcing their intention of returning to their former habits of exploitation and luxury. Juan, disheartened by their reaction, resolves to abandon his family unless they will cease their arrogance and will love and obey him of their own free choice. These conditions are accepted by his wife and daughter, and the play ends with little perceptible change in Juan's basic character, but with a promise that despite his weakness, Don Juan will now live with a sense of dignity.

As in his play *That's My Man,* Arniches again resorts to the use of disguise as a device to impose order on a domestic scene where discomfiture reigns due to the protagonist's inherent cowardice. Juan, with his kindly nature, his lack of self-confidence, and his unheroic abulia—a condition not unlike that which Ángel Ganivet proposed as being Spain's greatest weakness—is a facsimile of Antonio's pusillanimous disposition. And as is the case with his model, Don Juan's pretended strength also serves to reduce the play's action to a sad and paradoxical lesson, that the esteem of others is not gained through acts of kindness and love, but by assuming an authoritative posture. Indeed, it is Juan's bitter contention that "we do not respect those who love us, but rather those who terrify us."

To the exclusion of his other characters, who for the most part remain mere stereotypes, Arniches concentrates all of his artistry on the delineation of Don Juan. A single flaw in Juan's personality is the source of the play's improbable events, yet in his unsuccessful struggle to overcome this flaw, Juan himself remains a unified and consistent character. In keeping with a characteristic pattern of the grotesque tragedies, the protagonist's weakness is insurmountable to the very end, and leads to an unheroic compromise rather than a tragic fall.

V *Other Grotesque Tragedies*

Within a period of four years (1930–1933), Arniches wrote five major plays within the formula of the grotesque tragedy. Two of them he labeled with tags of a different description—*El señor Badanas (Mr. Badanas)* was called a tragicomedy; *Vivir de ilusiones (Living on Dreams)*, a comic farce—yet both are as faithful to the essential notion of the genre as anything he wrote. Owing to their importance in contributing to the distinction of Arniches' theater during the productive penultimate decade of his life, each of these five dramas will be discussed in terms of their relationship to the defined concept of the grotesque tragedy.

Bearing a title reminiscent of Rubén Darío's "Sonatina" and satirizing the elegant frivolity of high society somewhat in the manner of Jacinto Benavente's formula for high comedy, Arniches' fourth grotesque tragedy, *La condesa está triste (The Countess Is Sad)*, censures the superficiality and corruption of Madrid's hypocritical aristocracy.

The action centers around the love of an aging widow for a shrewd young man whose only interest is in her wealth. The Countess has two daughters, one of whom is involved in a liaison with a wealthy suitor twice her age, whose only intent is to seduce her. The other, Gloria, is a typical heroine of good breeding who is incensed to learn that her mother and sister are dragging the family's good name through the mire. Gloria's fiancé discovers that the Countess' intended is deceiving her, for he is already married and has two children, with a third on the way. When the Countess verifies the fraud, she is overwhelmed with grief. This has been the first genuine love of her life, for each of her former unions had been a marriage of convenience.

In the end the Countess stands as a solitary and pathetic figure, acknowledging that in her foolish effort to resist growing old by taking a young lover, she has only deceived herself. Her tragedy is the grotesqueness of a passion for a handsome dandy whose pretense of affection has made the old woman look ridiculous in the eyes of her cherished social circle. The falseness of her make-believe world condemns her to live out her life in loneliness.

In *The Countess Is Sad* Arniches describes an aspect of contemporary Madrilenean society that is entirely opposite on the social scale to the world he portrays in *That's My Man*. In either case, however, the dénouement offers little assurance that matters will improve in the future. Antonio in his poverty and the Countess amid her affluence must live on in their respective situations to face their problems. This fact bears out Arniches' ever-recurring thought that every individual must strive to maintain, or to secure for the first time, his personal sense of dignity or rightful position in society, regardless of his social level.

Mr. Badanas, the next play of grotesque tragedy elements, revives the theme of the *pobre hombre* and sustains on a wide scale the social criticism apparent in *The Countess Is Sad*. The protagonist is yet another victim of unauthenticity. Responding to the ambitions of his wife and her brother, Saturiano Badanas feigns a tough exterior to hide a natural timidity and thereby climbs from the inferior ranks of an insignificant administrative post to become General Director of Highways. His feigned firmness of character leads him to the acquisition of national honors and medals of distinction, but at the price of sacrificing a kindly co-worker by an act of malice.

Though Badanas is troubled throughout the play by a sense of regret over the lie he must live if he is to command respect, it is not until a good human being nears the brink of suicide as the helpless victim of his misdeeds that he feels true pangs of remorse. He ultimately repudiates the sham, recognizing that the perverse ambitions of others had obliged him to play a role for which he was ill suited. A summary of the plot fails to convey the humorous tone that veils much of the serious impact of the play. The pretense that Saturiano Badanas maintains gives rise to a whole series of improbable happenings and situations which, by virtue of their farcical spirit, create a grotesque atmosphere charged with humor. The code of false values to which Badanas clings in his easy ascendancy to political power is itself a source of exaggerated comedy, and

affords Arniches an opportunity to lampoon hypocrisy in bureau-
cratic procedures and to satirize social manners.

The following year Arniches staged a compelling drama in which
a deliberate act of duplicity, identical to the spirit of the deceptions
dramatized in the aforenamed plays, is maintained to protect an
old woman from the shock of facing the anachronism of her in-
transigent ideas. *Vivir de ilusiones (Living on Dreams)* concerns
the pathetic world of fantasy that a highborn but impoverished
widow harbors as the sole comfort of her broken heart.

Doña Leonor de Talavera yearns for the day when she will
marry her daughter to a wealthy aristocrat and gain perhaps a
similar prize for herself. Her daughter is engaged to a commoner
from the working class, but in deference to the kind old lady's
dream and last grip on hope, the two young people, with the aid
of the fiancé's mother, invent a merciful kind of farce in which the
widow is made to believe that the gentleman in question has
descended from an English duke. Arniches concludes the action by
having the old woman recover her sense of reality. She recognizes
in the end that true nobility is found not in a declining or decadent
bloodline, but in one's honest dealings with his fellowmen.

The widow's make-believe world belongs to the broad concept
of the grotesque tragedy in the same way that Florita's misadventures in *Miss Trevélez* conform to the genre; that is, her predicament borders on tragedy but elicits genuine laughter. The difference, however, is that Flora is the victim of a cruel joke while
Doña Leonor's deceivers spare her from embitterment. The earlier
play is rooted in the plausible context of human sadness and is
funny only because of its dialogue; *Living on Dreams* is intentionally
overplayed as a comedy of situation and could well have degenerated
into a sentimental melodrama were it not for the author's highly
developed sense of comic exaggeration. In this connection Luis
Calvo is correct in affirming that Arniches avails himself of caricature
to avoid falling into melodrama.[8]

The conflict arising out of the clash between dream and reality
also forms the nucleus of *La diosa ríe (The Goddess Laughs)*,
a play that Ramos has praised as being comparable to any of the
most celebrated of Arniches' grotesque tragedies.[9] The action
revolves around the blind and hopeless passion of Paulino, a
humble store employee, for Rosita del Oro, a famous stage actress.
Paulino has paid court to his "goddess" by sending her flowers and

letters. Rosita, impelled by curiosity and in search of an idyllic and pure romance, visits the store in which Paulino works with the pretext of buying a pair of gloves. She presents her enamored friend with a ticket to view her benefit performance. Paulino, overjoyed with the prospect that his fondest dream might come true, first buys a new suit with money he had lifted from the cash register, then helps himself to an expensive watch as a gift for Rosita. Paulino is a conspicuous and grotesque figure among the high social set of the theater, but Rosita is moved by his devotion and senses an awakening of genuine love in her heart. She decides thereupon to visit his family.

The boy's mother, a sensible and protective matron, convinces Rosita that her world of luxury and fast entertainment is completely incompatible with Paulino's drab existence. Reality must prevail over their impossible dream. Consequently, the two agree to separate forever, Rosita returning to the theater, Paulino to the shop to repay his debts. The charming laughter of Paulino's goddess will continue to haunt him in the shape of a memory of their platonic relationship and a sigh over what might have been.

The Goddess Laughs illustrates Arniches' use of the grotesque to represent humorously a convincing albeit agonizing situation from everyday life. The young man's passion thrusts him into a dilemma from which any escape would appear ridiculous. His initial misfortune—falling in love with Rosita de Oro—is treated lightly, though it represents a crisis in his uneventful life. Rosita's involvement, however, complicates the farce, propelling a mere game of external comedy into the realm of profound gravity, the two polarities that Pedro Salinas has defined as constituting the essence of a grotesque tragedy.[10] While their separation verges upon heartache, the end result, prepared for by a constant overstatement of the catastrophe, is extremely humorous to the public.

Arniches' final grotesque tragedy, *El casto don José (Chaste Don José),* is the lightest and most comical play of the series. José is a middle-aged chocolate shop proprietor who attributes his staid and uncomplicated existence to a lifelong devotion to work and prayer, moderate personal habits, and a tranquil disposition. He lives in quiet mediocrity amidst the squalor of his unkempt shop and the base simplicity of his grooming. His accustomed serenity comes quickly to an end, however, when he grants his nephew Paquito, his only surviving relative, lodging in his house. Paquito first appears as a renegade; upon entering José's house he brings two strange women with him, asking that they be given protection. Shocked and indignant, José's housekeeper and her son, with the support of a pious old friend, urge the immediate expulsion of Paquito and the two female freeloaders. Hypocritically pretending to espouse charitable causes for their own advancement, José's old friends have designs on his modest fortune; they tell him that Paquito's presence poses a threat to Don José's chaste reputation, while in truth they fear Paquito might gain a legal control over his uncle's savings.

In spite of his timidity and frequent vacillations, Don José falls hopelessly in love with Doña Maravillas, one of the women who came to his house with Paquito. The leeches in his midst endeavor to dissuade him from inviting further scandal, but the effect of love has already rendered a complete transformation in José's once humble and retiring nature. He is now polished, clean, and self-assured. Moreover, he is angry to think that his trusted friends have had avaricious designs. When faced with the rumor that his beloved Doña Maravillas is deceiving him because she is already married, José loses his composure altogether and announces his intention to kill himself, for it is impossible for him to go on living without the woman who has brought him the only real happiness he has known. But at the crucial moment of his suicide attempt, Don José lacks the courage to pull the trigger. He emerges from his room pleading that someone else kill him. He then learns that the rumor of Doña Maravillas' marriage is false, that in reality she is a widow, free and willing to marry him. As part of the play's happy ending, José dismisses his false friends and welcomes Paquito into his household.

Due to its farcical and nontragic nature, Ramos judges *Chaste Don José* the least representative of the grotesque tragedies.[11] Yet in its prevailing optimistic tone, it is a drama of grotesque caricature in which an exaggerated sense of comedy serves to cover up a serious conflict, in this case Don José's struggle to assert himself in spite of the opposition of old comrades and his own vacillating and gullible nature.

It is apparent that the mere presence or absence of humor is not by itself a valid determining factor in the definition of a grotesque tragedy. Even in their most comical scenes, the plays we have discussed often appear bitter, while their most painful situations come across with a delicate touch of humor. The grotesque hero expounds his problems between laughter and tears, and ventures upon life now with pranks, now with pathos. For Arniches life is a combination of tragedy and comedy; his plays therefore juxtapose the two, and his characters are an amalgam of both. The serious problems he depicts are always shaded with comic situations. Only the end of a play will indicate which aspect, the tragic or the comic, is to prevail in the life of the protagonist. The key, then, to the effect of the grotesque tragedy lies in the figure of the grotesque hero, who never surrenders that fascinating composite of the pathetic and the ridiculous, the satiric and the ironic, the serious and the comic, which defines his burden with such an overtragic insistence that all of his actions and the dilemma itself can appear to be nothing less than grotesque.

VI *The Nature of the Grotesque Tragedy: An Outline Summary*

The following topics, presented by way of summary to the foregoing discussion, are offered as simple tags to enable the reader to grasp the notion of Carlos Arniches' most singular invention for the theater: the grotesque tragedy. These characteristics are germane to the entire collection of the plays under this classification; they are not to be considered invariable formulas applicable to each individual work, but as guidelines for distinguishing this genre from other varieties of theatrical offerings.

A. *The Grotesque Play*
1. The primary purpose is to entertain.
2. The plot presents a serious problem of life of everyday concern.
3. The conflict involves a character who is agonizing under the burden of his own enervated nature or struggling against a code of unrealistic values.
4. The action embodies a seriousness and an internal depth complementing the humor of the surface farce.
5. A chain of improbable episodes reduces the sense of verisimilitude.
6. Humorous dialogue and comic situations overlie serious, tragic, or sometimes catastrophic crises.
7. Caricature and overstatement are paramount to the action and to the characterization.
8. The dénouement settles the issue at hand but rarely resolves the protagonist's basic conflict.

9. A moral lesson is apparent and is often stated explicitly at the end of the play.
10. The action is generally suited to convey an optimistic view of life; good triumphs over evil.

B. *The Grotesque Hero*

1. He does not perish or suffer an ignominious defeat.
2. He has an obvious character flaw that he often conceals under a false pose.
3. He is frequently a sponger, or at least dependent on others for moral support.
4. He often becomes enmeshed in a bizarre, pathetic, or foolish predicament, the extrication from which tends to heighten the absurdity of his situation without resolving his basic problem.
5. His weaknesses are overstressed for comic effect, but his resistance to cynicism and remorse precludes our viewing his depiction as cruel.
6. His kind nature and sense of humor enable him to laugh at and to live with his own mistakes.
7. He appears both tragic and comic at the same time.
8. His triumph, if any, is restricted to a simple recognition of the worth and limitations of his existence.

CHAPTER 7

Two "Rapid Sainetes"

WHEN he was fifty years of age, Carlos Arniches released for publication eleven unique sketches he called his "rapid sainetes." They had appeared earlier on the pages of *Blanco y Negro,* one of Madrid's most popular periodicals. Under the single title *From the Soul of Madrid,* they were republished in 1917 as a simple gesture of Arniches' love for his adopted city. Owing to their brevity and charm and the exquisite freshness of their language and characterizations, the "rapid sainetes" provide an excellent compact example of Arniches' concern for the human emotions which lie beneath the calloused exterior of a Madrilenean *chulo,* or the stoical love for life to be found among the city's beggars and thieves.

Two of the best sainetes from the collection are translated on the following pages. Their humor and fast dialogue combine with the author's unmistakable moralistic view of human nature to depict a poignant slice of life from Madrid's Latin district. The characters are from the lower class; in their small joys and sorrows we encounter the living themes of many of Arniches' theatrical works. We note with interest the setting of each play's action: *The Atheists* takes place in the oldest sector of Madrid, amid dim, weathered edifices and dirty streets, where today's tourists are disinclined to enter unless it be on a Sunday jaunt to the Rastro in quest of a bargain at the flea market. Eulalio's humiliation in the first scene occurs in a tavern on Peñón Street, a name no longer found in modern guide books or on updated maps of the city, yet the street itself still stands as perhaps the most typical byway of an Arnichesian world. By official edict of the Municipal Government of Madrid in the year 1930, the name Peñón was changed to Carlos Arniches Street, a lasting tribute to the man who situated the action of most of his plays in the apartment flats, courtyards, taverns, and environs of the narrow street. Indeed, upon this very back street Ramón de la Cruz extracted scenes and types for several of his sainetes, and Goya discovered subjects for his magnificent etchings and paintings. Old Peñón Street is itself a museum of *costumbrismo.*

The conversations recorded in *The Paupers* take place one-quarter mile to the west of Peñón Street near the present-day María Cristina Hospital, just five hundred yards east over the railroad tracks from the Manzanares River. This area was one of Madrid's appalling slums when Arniches wrote his engaging "rapid sainete," a playlet teeming with mendicant street gossip. It was here that many destitute beggars gathered to plan their assault on the moneyed districts to the north. And it was here that many of society's offscourings sought companionship among their own kind, retreating betimes from the hostile, uncharitable world of Alcalá, Castellana, and the Gran Vía. Among those unwashed ragamuffins from whom he often snatched genuine gleanings of humanity, Arniches invites us to pause and heed the complaints and dreams of a handful of artful professional beggars.

We are deprived of a special enchantment of local color in an English translation of any of Arniches' plays, particularly his sainetes of Madrilenean customs. Heretofore, the only English version of a "rapid sainete" was that published in 1934 by Willis Knapp Jones, whose translation of *The Philosophic Cobbler* appears in *Spanish One-Act Plays in English* (Dallas: Tardy). In reading the Jones translation, as good as it is, we are painfully aware that a vital force is missing; a play which drew its vitality from the inimitable vernacular of Madrilenean speech has somehow been reduced to banality. Admittedly, despite our own assiduous choice of colloquial expressions and colorful English jargon, rendered occasionally with substandard orthography and grammar, there remains a void which only the language of the original composition could fill. At best the effort underscores the significance of Cervantes' derogatory comment on translating from one tongue into another, which he likens to our viewing Flemish tapestries from the wrong side, "for although you see the pictures, they are covered with threads which obscure them so that the smoothness and gloss of the fabric are lost." It is a deluded view of reality, but we cling to the hope that in some way the charm so characteristic of Arniches' writings will be conveyed in these translations.

THE ATHEISTS

Scene One

Interior of a tavern located on Peñón Street near the Plaza del Campillo de Mundo Nuevo.

It is evening. The barroom air, heavy with cigarette smoke, dims the glow of the weakened light bulbs, casting a sinister aspect upon the hungry and ragged people seated at the tables. A smell of wine, tobacco, and strongly seasoned food prevails.

At a corner table we find BALDOMERO *"The Squint-eyed,"* NICOMEDES *"The Sullen,"* EULALIO, *and* FLORO. *They have just eaten a light meal and are now engaged in a hand of cards.* PEPE OF MÁLAGA, *the proprietor, treats each of them to a small glass of wine.*

Boisterous chatter is heard concerning a recent goring in the bullring. Suddenly, somewhat indistinctly, the distant sound of the small bell on a funeral wagon is heard, tolling slowly and solemnly in the silent street. The ringing is followed by the heavy rumbling of wheels.

Within the tavern there is a brief pause of silence. Everyone's attention is directed to the sound outside. EULALIO, *with some indecision, lifts a hand dissemblingly and touches the visor of his cap. A loud outburst of laughter, giving rise in turn to a display of exaggerated astonishment, grimaces of mockery and coarse remarks, is the response the gathering offers to the poor old man's inoffensive gesture of respect.*

FLORO: *(In a fit of laughter.)* Ha, ha, ha! . . . Well, he damn near took it off! Ha, ha, ha! . . .

EULALIO: *(A little embarrassed.)* I was just . . .

BALDOMERO: Come on, take it off, ya pious ol' lady!

EULALIO: Look, fellas, just 'cuz a guy does somethin' on account he's got certain convictions, ain't no cause to . . .

NICOMEDES: We had you pegged for a common laborer, not a sanctimonious ol' woman! . . . Ha, ha, ha! . . .

PEPE: For half a century he has us thinkin' he breakfasts on acolytes in giblet fricassee, an' suddenly he turns out to be a believer!

EULALIO: Come on, would ya kindly lay off the insults!

FLORO: Eulalio, you're on the road to zealotry!

EULALIO: *(Now provoked.)* I'm on my way to another bar! You watch it, friend, or in short order your nose is gonna contend with my fist!

FLORO: *(Pounding his fist on the table.)* Well, then, what's the idea payin' homage to those ecclesiastic humbugs, eh?

EULALIO: I show my respect 'cuz I don't think a slight gesture can do any harm. It ain't that I'm a churchgoer—God save me from that!—but I ain't like you neither, like that time ya sneezed on the street and some guy said "God bless you!" an' ya took'm to task for't. An' I ain't like that fellow over there who can't pass by a priest without sayin' an offensive word or makin' a gesture. Sure, I don't cross myself an' I don't believe in those stupid saints and nine-day devotions . . . but by heaven, ya gotta have a little smidgen o' faith in something . . .

FLORO: Faith in human progress!

THE ENTIRE GROUP: *(Now absorbed in the argument.)* Right! There y'are!

EULALIO: Oh, I've got faith in that. But what I'm tryin' to tell ya, Floro, there's gotta be a Supreme Being, call'm God or what'cha want, a being who created this here universe around us.

FLORO: Here there ain't no other God or no other being 'cept Mother Nature an' her product: man . . . a free an' sovereign animal. An' beyond that, ya might's well talk to me of seasoned carrots.

EULALIO: Ya mean to tell me ya think the world was made by itself?

FLORO: Sure. An' why not?

EULALIO: An' just how'd that come about?

FLORO: It come out o' chaos.

EULALIO: *(Doubting.)* Chaos, hooey, ya don't know what you're talkin' about.

FLORO: Nothin' more nor less. Out o' chaos.

EULALIO: An' what do ya mean by chaos?

FLORO: A lot o' nothingness floatin' around.

NICOMEDES: *(Admiringly.)* Ha! He ain't gonna get hooked!

FLORO: An' just so you'll learn somethin' you're ignorant about, I'm gonna tell ya that this here terrestrial globe we live on ain't nothin' more nor less than a hunk that's broke off another planet.

A LISTENER: Bull.

FLORO: *(Very irritated.)* Who said that? Let him step up here an' I'll belt him in the face with this bottle.

SEVERAL VOICES: Quiet! . . . Take it easy! . . . *(A profound silence.)*

EULALIO: Okay, tell me, then . . . what am *I*, huh?

FLORO: You? You're a miserable worm devoted to bricklayin' an' formed o' terrestrial crap.

EULALIO: Hey! You callin' me a worm? Watch it, Floro, you're sayin' some things that ain't . . .

FLORO: Ah, simmer down . . . Look, I'll prove to ya what I mean. Here's a practical example of your worminess. Ya take this here piece o' cheese, toss it over in that there corner, come back in a couple o' weeks, an' you'll find it's rotted away.

EULALIO: Ha! That's 'cuz there ain't no rats. If you got rats ya won't find no cheese at all!

FLORO: Well, here they gotta cat. That's the reason I'm givin' ya the example. So, in the same way the piece o' cheese rots away an' the worms an' other crawlin' vermin come out, so out o' the shell of this here world come people . . . worms! . . . an' that's you an' me an' him an' him an' Ignacia, Tadea, an' all them women folk we live with.

ALL: Very good! Bravo!

A LISTENER: That ain't possible, Floro.

FLORO: An' who the hell's croakin' out that objection?

THE LISTENER: Me. If I believed for a minute that a woman with the eyes an' the shape of your sister-in-law could be the result of a hunk o' cheese, I'd toss in the towel! *(The others all laugh.)*

FLORO: *(Angrily.)* You've got a head, my friend, that if put in a melon stall, would compare damn good with the other fruit. I'm philosophizin', see? An' for that reason I'm talkin' in a hypothecary sense.

THE LISTENER: Well, in that case . . . 'scuse me . . .

FLORO: Forget it. It jus' takes one little ear to hear with. Now then, let me finish. Okay, Eulalio, there just ain't no such thing as a supreme being, nor a heaven, nor a purgatory, nor any o' that sorta nonsense. In this world there ain't nothin' more than this world, where ya find it all . . . the good, the bad, an' the in-between. An' the day ya die, ya go back to the bosom of mother earth an' there ya become dust, phosphorus, fizzy water . . . nothin'. So there!

Delirious applause and coarse laughter greet the atheist's last words. EULALIO, reduced to silence by the explosive dialectics of his adversary, sits quietly in a corner.

Once again the small bell from the distant funeral wagon is heard as the vehicle draws near on its return. At last it goes by, and the sound is eventually lost in the silence of the deserted street, followed by the slow rolling of the wheels.

In spite of all that has transpired, the poor people of the tavern have ceased laughing.

Scene Two

Interior of a humble bedroom in a poor dwelling. It is two o'clock in the morning. The ticktock of a clock is heard in the darkness.

FLORO, the implacable atheist, and his wife FELIPA, are asleep on a modest bed. Suddenly the poor man awakens, gives a sharp cry, and grabs the left side of his chest. He straightens up, livid and trembling.

FLORO: Ayyy! Ay, Felipa!

FELIPA: *(Awakens, filled with terror.)* What's wrong, Floro? *(She turns on the light.)*

FLORO: Ay, Felipa . . . the pain . . . what a terrible pain! Ayyy, I'm dying . . . !

FELIPA: But, what's happening to you?

FLORO: Ay, I don't know . . . It's as if I had a dagger in me . . . !

FELIPA: *(Climbing out of bed.)* But where?

FLORO: Ay! Here! . . . Ay, get a doctor . . . I can't breathe! . . . Ay, Felipa, it's a pain in my side . . . ! Ay, I don't know what's the matter . . . !

FELIPA: For God's sake, Floro, lie still!

Suffering from an intense intercostal neuralgia, FLORO *continues complaining with bitter laments while* FELIPA *hurriedly dresses and runs to call the neighbors.*

The room soon fills with half-dressed people, who scurry from one end to the other, perplexed and stupefied.

FIRST NEIGHBOR: What happened?

SECOND NEIGHBOR: Floro, what's wrong?

THIRD NEIGHBOR: Must be something that doesn't agree with him.

FOURTH NEIGHBOR: What'd you eat last night?

FLORO: Ay, I don't remember . . . Oh, I'm dyin'! Help me, for the love of heaven.

A VOICE: It must have been the tuna fish!

ANOTHER: It could be gas.

STILL ANOTHER: Get him some tea.

YET ANOTHER: Give him oil.

FIRST NEIGHBOR: Put him over on his stomach.

SECOND NEIGHBOR: Get'm a warm blanket.

FELIPA: Matthew, for God's sake, run down to the clinic and get a doctor.

MATTHEW: I'm on my way. *(He rushes out.)*

The ill man is brought boiling water, ointments, thick flannel blankets, warm bricks . . . all to no avail. His violence does not subside. In a paroxysm of pain, FLORO *utters desperate and frightful cries while twisting convulsively on the bed.*

FLORO: Ay, I'm dying . . . ! Ayyy, I can't go on . . . ! Virgin of Carmen, relieve me of this pain . . . . Help me! Oh, blessed God . . . !

DOÑA ESCOLÁSTICA, *an old woman considered by the neighborhood to be overly pious, draws near the bed.*

DOÑA ESCOLA: Listen, Floro, because you have your own ideas, I haven't dared say anything to you. . . . But now that I hear you mention God and the Holy Virgin, if you wish, I'll give you a remedy that will remove your pain in two seconds.

FLORO: *(Sitting up. He looks at her anxiously.)* In two seconds? *(Clasping her.)* Ay, my dear Doña Escola, tell me, by your mother, come what may, before I die!

DOÑA ESCOLA: I have a few small stamps of the Virgin of the Paloma, you understand? You roll them up real small, make them like a ball, swallow them with a sip of water. Then offer a prayer in faith and you'll be cured at once!

FLORO: *(Looking at her with anguish.)* Ay, Doña Escola . . . ay! I'm not able to do it!

DOÑA ESCOLA: But why not?

FLORO: My . . . ideas. They just won't let me do it.

DOÑA ESCOLA: But don't you see that if you die, you won't be left with a single one of your ideas!

FLORO: Ay, Doña Escola, don't force me to depart from my creed . . . to believe in nothin'!

DOÑA ESCOLA: Well, that's some lousy creed!

FELIPA: Please, Floro, take the stamps. They say that miraculous things have occurred!

FLORO: Ay, but I can't! Anything but that!

DOÑA ESCOLA: But what has the Virgin of the Paloma ever done to you?

FLORO: It isn't the Virgin, it's my friend Lerroux who would give me hell if he ever found out.

LERROUX: An' just who's goin' to tell me?

DOÑA ESCOLA: Hurray! Bring water . . . here's the holy stamp . . . swallow it.

FELIPA: Drink it with faith, Floro.

FLORO: Ay! All right . . . I'll take it 'cuz I can't stand the pain no longer; but, by God, don't say nothin' about this to Pablo Iglesias, or he'll never speak to me again.

DOÑA ESCOLA: Open up.

FLORO: *(After swallowing the stamp.)* Ay, there . . . it's done. Ay, Holy Virgin, forgive me for all I've done to offend you. But remove this awful pain that is piercing my body, an' as soon as I get up I'll make a wax bricklayer an' bring it to ya! . . .

He gives a great sigh. The moans are progressively diminishing. Soon he falls asleep. The women pray softly.

Scene Three

EULALIO *is strolling along Ventosa Street. Upon turning the corner at Paloma Street he stops in his tracks, seeing* FLORO *approach with an uncertain gait and dark circles under his eyes.* FLORO *is returning from church and carries a long, thick candle in his hand, half covered with newspaper.*

EULALIO: *(Detaining him.)* Good mornin', Floro!

FLORO: *(Terrified.)* Eulalio! *(He doesn't know what to do with his candle.)*

EULALIO: *(Smiling.)* What do ya have in your hand?

FLORO: Nothin'. On my way to work some of the women in my neighborhood asked me to take this silly thing over to that stupid church on the . . .

EULALIO: *(Widening his smile.)* Don't bother. . . . I know all about it!

FLORO: They told you about my pain last night?

EULALIO: Yeah, an' all about the little stamp.

FLORO: *(Lowering his head with shame.)* Eulalio, ol' fellow, it's true. They made me eat crow . . . but I was in such a bad way. I thought sure I was a goner. An' when a guy is starin' straight into the face of death . . . !

EULALIO: You don't have to say no more, Floro! I was once worse off than you! Why, with regard to atheism, I could have beat your arguments by twenty-five to fifty percent. But, my friend, one day—you know how I feel about my granddaughter. There's nothin' else I love more in this here world . . . well, I came down with what they call diphtheria, an' I thought for sure I was goin' to die. Man! Just the thought that I was goin' to be deprived of that angelic little girl who grabs me around the knees every evening when I return home from work, and who is my only comfort . . . let me tell ya, it brought me such anguish in here, deep inside, that I said, "Lord, if you'll but save me, I'll wear the cloth no matter what!" An' He saved me! For that reason, last night, in the tavern, when the funeral wagon went by, I went to take off my cap. One's gotta be grateful.

FLORO: You're right, Eulalio. Please forgive me for those stupid things I said to ya.

EULALIO: Never mind, ol' buddy; I understand. When a man is well an' healthy an' finds himself in a tavern surrounded by four fools who will sneer at anything, that man is strong; he'll dare to challenge all that's human and all that's divine. But when the wind changes an' the dark hour comes, an' pain makes him frightened an' he's all alone in a corner of his house, . . . regardless of his impiety, that man, I tell ya, will raise his eyes to heaven an' plead for mercy.

FLORO: Ain't that the truth.

EULALIO: Anyhow, would ya believe that I even cross myself at night?

FLORO: *(With amazement.)* Ya still remember to?

EULALIO: Why, mister, that's the first thing your mother teaches ya. An' I do more than that.

FLORO: What is it?

EULALIO: Whenever I go by a church I cross myself, an' if my friends are lookin', I take off my beret an' I shake it as if to remove bits o' plaster.

FLORO: I've always lifted the visor o' my cap an' scratched my head.

EULALIO: Yeah, but that ain't nothin' new.

FLORO: Ya don't think so?

EULALIO: Naw, I seen that done by hundreds of atheists.

Curtain

The Paupers

*Those of you who have compassionate feelings and magnanimous hearts,
who yield to the mournful plaints of the beggar as he extends his frail hand
to you on the street: follow me. Come with me to the filthy corners of a sad
and miserable, insidious and debauched Madrid which, fortunately, you have
yet to discover; and listen to the following dialogues that are as edifying
as they are true.*

*We are on Gilimón Street. It is a clear and cold afternoon. The sky is blue
and the sun is bright.*

Two neighbors, Señora GALA *and "Squint-eyed"* PETRA, *have just made a
public display of their differences with bites, blows, scratchings, and vile
insults before a ragged and jubilant crowd. The fight ends and the squabblers
withdraw, each accompanied by her supporters, to repair their wounds.
The tumult gradually subsides.*

*Next to the wall of the Hospital of the Third Order, huddled together in the
sunlight, are two tattered old women,* LIBRADA *and* JUSTA. *Near them is
"Bad-luck"* CELIPE, *an old man, seated on a box. He is removing tobacco
from a pile of cigarette butts in order to refashion his own.* PENDINGUE,
*the knife grinder, is busy polishing a cobbler's shears. Farther away a group
of youngsters play with considerable ruckus.*

JUSTA: What was the scuffle all about?

LIBRADA: Best to say it ain't ended yet.

JUSTA: But what is ol' Squinty bitchin' about?

LIBRADA: I'll tell ya! Gala still owes her a month's wages for the kids. It's a
real mess.

JUSTA: Oh! Ya mean to say she's hired out her kids?

LIBRADA: For the last month an' a half! An' for a peseta fifty a day. One
peseta for the oldest an' fifty cents for the little guy. It's a steal, 'cuz you
oughta see how well that child can beg.

JUSTA: I've heard he's a gem.

LIBRADA: Why, there ain't a night goes by that he don't come in with over
three pesetas. An' he deserves every bit he gets . . . he's mighty sharp,
that one. Turn 'im loose on Alcalá Street, he sees a young attractive
girl with one of those fancy-garbed ol' men, an' the next thing ya know
he's grabbin' hold of the ol' boy's coattail, and says to him: "Alms,
my good sir, for the health of your lady, who is very lovely. You should
buy her a car, she has such beautiful eyes . . . buy her one, sir." Then
they look down on him an' laugh an' the gentleman'll say, "What a
cute little waif!" An' she'll say, "He's so darling!" An' there's not a
couple that won't part with at least two or three coins.

JUSTA: What a clever lad!

LIBRADA: An' ya oughta see the oldest!

JUSTA: That brat?

LIBRADA: Call 'im what you want, my dear, but he's a child wonder. He takes a little basket, see? An' an empty bottle, then he goes to a busy street corner an' sits on the pavement. Then he starts weepin' so bitter like, you'd think his poor little heart's breakin', an' when he gets a good group o' people gathered 'round 'im, then ya oughta hear 'im! "Ay, my poor mother! Ayyy! We ain't had nothin' to eat for two days! . . . She give me two pesetas to buy oil with, an' on my way I lost 'em! Ay, I can't go back home again. My poor father is so sick! Ay, if only he had some food to eat!" An' then all the people are so moved hearin' the little guy carry on so, they take up a collection then an' there . . . an' there ain't a sob session that don't bring that kid at least five or six coins.

JUSTA: Well, you just gotta say them there two kids are gold mines!

LIBRADA: They bring in more'n a pawnshop. An' speakin' o' beggin', ya know who else gets more'n her share o' the take?

JUSTA: Who?

LIBRADA: Doña Encarnación, the one over on San Bernabé Street.

JUSTA: Doña Encarnación . . . Doña Encarnación. I just don't place her.

LIBRADA: Come on, my dear, don't be so dumb. The one that begs dressed in mournin', with the long cloak. She covers her face and it seems that her voice is comin' out of a cistern.

JUSTA: Oh, sure! . . . An' you say she makes a lot of money?

LIBRADA: You bet she wouldn't cut off a finger for less than six thousand pesetas.

JUSTA: Goodness; but I've heard people say she goes into high society.

LIBRADA: Yep, she begs only in the high-class churches an' at the exits of first-rate taverns or theaters or the most fashionable nightclubs. Whenever she sees a real lady she gives her dandiest performance. She goes up to her and she says in a loud voice so's all the people 'round 'em will hear: "Madam Marquesa, I am ravenous. I would appreciate your ladyship's granting me a small obolus."

JUSTA: What's an obolus?

LIBRADA: Damned if I know, but it must be somethin' expensive; you see, that's where she's real clever. I think she'd say "Your ladyship" to a wet nurse.

JUSTA: Land sake, just think what some people know.

LIBRADA: She got her knowin' from royalty. At one time she was a real important lady. In them days she didn't get drunk an' her manners were second to none. I've been told she's the daughter of a rancher from Chinchón.

JUSTA: Well, at least that's the impression she gives.

LIBRADA: Her speakin's very polite. Whenever she sees me she calls me squalid. An' I don't know what that means neither.

JUSTA: Probably somethin' exquisite.

LIBRADA: I'll say. When she says it . . .

JUSTA: Ya don't beg no longer at San Ginés, do ya, Librada?

LIBRADA: No, my dear. I had words with the sacristan an' I ain't gone back. Too much riffraff over there. I've now taken up with Pelitos an' we've been doin' the part of shy beggars.

JUSTA: Ya makin' good at it?

LIBRADA: Well, my dear, all things considerin', we're gettin' by. But it ain't easy. Just for instance, the inspector from San Vicente calls at my house; there you have me takin' all my furniture over to Pelitos' house. I'm left with a straw bed, an ol' trunk, half a candle in a bottle, an' a broken chair. We bed Casimiro down—you know, Onofra's little boy. He's an expert at coughs and moans. We put on such a show that it'd break the heart of the meanest beast. An' then, just to give ya another example, the social worker goes over to Pelitos' house, an' he's gotta climb over all my household stuff, then my friend Cosme, he gets wrapped up in a blanket an' pretends to be dyin', enough to scare ya outta your wits, an' there ain't a day goes by that the 'spector doesn't leave us three or four pesetas outta his own pocket in addition to our weekly pension.

JUSTA: So that's why you're all stuffin' yourselves with pickled salads an' wine.

LIBRADA: An' don't you think one deserves all she can get in the battle of wits with those crafty old ladies who ask ya for a receipt for every small coin they give away?

CELIPE: *(Joining in the conversation.)* Ya can say that again. Ya oughta see how awful charity's come to be nowadays. It stinks. Why, just the other day, when I went out to beg, this lady starts givin' me hell. If there hadn't been other people around, I'd have belted her.

JUSTA: What happened?

CELIPE: Oh, nothin'. I just take off my cap an' say in such a tone o' pain it'd split a rock, "Lady, for the health o' your children, gimme somethin' to buy a little bit o' bread, for I ain't had nothin' for two days." Well, she pays me no attention an' ups an' scampers away. "Lady," I says, "I'm in terrible need. If ya ain't disposed to give it on trust, over there's a bakery shop. Ya can buy it for me there." So then we go an' she buys me this here loaf o' bread, see? Then out we go, an'—would'ya believe it?—she ups an' breaks it in two parts afore givin' it to me!

LIBRADA: What a mean ol' bitch!

JUSTA: Just so's ya won't go an' resell it, eh?

CELIPE: Yeah, an' that's exactly what I was about to do afore she mutilated it. They're all shameless hussies.

LIBRADA: I would o' smacked the stupid . . .

CELIPE: Forget it. I know her kind . . .

JUSTA: An' the handkerchief gag . . . is it payin' off, Celipe?

CELIPE: Still our most profitable, but it's been fallin' off lately.

LIBRADA: An' what's this handkerchief gag?

CELIPE: Ain't nothin' much, a little trick Quintín thought up. He's one helluva inventor. He went an' recruited these seven or eight friends o' his from off the hill an' from aroun' Descargas; then he marks us up as bricklayers with a little piece o' plaster, so's it looks like we just come down off a scaffold. Then he takes us up to Recoletos, he spreads out this here big handkerchief in the middle o' the sidewalk, then he points to us, sayin' all the while to everybody passin' by, "Group o' workmen laid off the job!"

LIBRADA: An' did ya take in a lot?

CELIPE: There was one day when we got up to six-eighty a person, not countin' the supper, wine, an' cigars. But the other day, when there were seventeen of us, we spread out the handkerchief on Castellana an'. . . not a damn thing! Not even fifteen cents . . . an' even the President of the Council come by. He didn't leave us nothin' but some swell encouragement.

PENDIGUE: *(Throwing his sharpening tools upon his back.)* Ahh, after listenin' to all o' you I think it's amazin' there're still such fools like me still workin' for a livin'.

CELIPE: What's eatin' ya, Pendigue?

PENDIGUE: You're all a bunch o' scoundrels! They'd do well to round you all up an' toss ya into the poorhouse.

CELIPE: Round us up! Ha! Ha! An' don't you think they've tried doin' that lots o' times! Why, the mayor himself says it's a hopeless task.

LIBRADA: Besides, if they didn't give us alms, we wouldn't have to beg!

JUSTA: Amen! By jingle, if they want to do away with beggin' on the streets an' they wanna round somebody up, it ain't us paupers who go beggin' they need to round up, they should round up all the stupid people who give alms. They're the guilty ones!

CELIPE: Damn right!

PENDIGUE: Say, now, ain't that the truth. When I run into the mayor, I'll tell him so myself! *(He leaves.)*

CELIPE: An' give him our affectionate regards.

Curtain

CHAPTER 8

Summation

CARLOS Arniches devoted his entire life to bearing witness to the goodness of man and the worth of human endeavor. He found a fruitful source for his revelation of the joys and sorrows of common people in the simple lives of his fellow Madrilenean citizens, who provided the background, warmth, and color for most of his plays. Their influence on the playwright was repaid in kind, for over the fifty-five years of his sustained triumphs for the Spanish stage, Arniches enriched Madrilenean speech with new or transformed words and phrases, while producing in the process a legacy of high literary value to immortalize the folk customs and the vital wisdom of the city's people.

The author's own words, uttered one year before his death, serve best to sum up the mission of his life and work: "I, by profession and by choice, have always wished to live in contact with the common soul of the Spanish people. And by this proximity of their soul with mine, I have been able to perceive the why and the wherefore of all the arbitrary, contradictory, picturesque, and complicated conditions which lie in the very heart of the Spanish soul."[1]

"His teachings," observed Pérez Minik a few years ago, "have arrived with freshness to our time, and his critical and human understanding of our society, especially of the middle and lower classes, has now merged with other present-day concerns and manners, lending a living quality to his permanence and influence."[2] In a strictly literary sense, Arniches paved the way for such playwrights as Enrique Jardiel Poncela, Miguel Mihura, Edgar Neville, and Alfonso Paso to conceive and to realize many of their great stage successes. The Spanish theater of today is indebted to his professional example and to the clarity of his dramatic expression.

In reflecting upon Arniches' long life and his decisive role in the evolution of modern Spanish drama, one is reminded of a fitting passage from Chapter 30 of *The Web and the Rock* by Thomas Wolfe: "If a man has a talent and learns somehow to use the whole of it, he has gloriously succeeded, and won a satisfaction and a triumph few men ever know."

114

Notes and References

Preface

1. The figure 191 includes all known published and inedited works for the stage plus twelve "rapid *sainetes*" written for reading pleasure only. Arniches exaggerated his own contribution to the theater by placing the number at three hundred. A few critics have perpetuated this overstatement. Alfredo Marquerie, for instance, states that Arniches wrote 282 plays, José Monleón sets the number at 270, and Juan Emilio Aragonés attributes over two hundred writings to the playwright. Major bibliographies also vary considerably. Romo Arregui gives only 157 titles, Portillo increases that figure by ten, and Juliá Martínez contributes an equally scanty listing. Vicente Ramos and Manfred Lentzen, however, come closest to the correct figure with 172 and 178 titles, respectively.

2. It will be observed hereafter that such common Spanish theater terms and genre names as sainete, zarzuela, entremés, and paso, owing to their frequent repetition in this study, will not be italicized. Each of these terms will be defined in its appropriate context.

3. A thorough study of the phonetic, morphological, and lexicographic features of Madrid's dialect as seen in the works of Arniches is found in a doctoral thesis by Francisco Trinidad, "A Study of Madrid's Dialect in Arniches' Plays" (University of California: Los Angeles, 1969).

Chapter One

1. Vicente Ramos, *Vida y teatro de Carlos Arniches* (Madrid: Alfaguara, 1966), p. 21.

2. Arniches, "Recuerdo," in *El Correo* (Alicante, July 1, 1923).

3. *Ibid.*

4. From an interview with Arniches recorded in *El Día* (Alicante, December 12, 1921). See Ramos, *op cit.,* p. 119.

5. Ramos, pp. 30–31.

6. See Serafín Adame Martínez, "Arniches debe una peseta desde hace treinta y ocho años," in *Blanco y Negro,* No. 1826 (Madrid, May 16, 1926).

7. Ramos, p. 137.

8. *Ibid.,* p. 251. The other recipients were Pablo Casals, Juan de la Cierva, Manuel Saborido, and Valeriano León.

9. Alfredo Marquerie, *Veinte años de teatro en España* (Madrid: Editora Nacional, 1959), pp. 52–53.

10. Ramos, p. 117.

11. "Autorretrato," in Arniches, *Teatro completo,* III (Madrid: Aguilar, 1948), pp. 10–11.

12. Ramos, p. 117.

13. A. Carmona, "El día de don Carlos Arniches," in *ABC* (Madrid, March 27, 1932).

14. E.M. del Portillo, "Prólogo biográficocrítico," in *Teatro completo,* I (Madrid: Aguilar, 1948), p. 20.

15. Adame Martínez, *loc. cit.*

16. E. Chicote, *Cuando Fernando VII gastaba paletó* (Madrid: Reus, 1952), p. 97.

17. Miguel Mihura, *Obras completas* (Barcelona: AHR, 1962), p. 25.

18. Stated by Valeriano León over Radio Nacional de España, April, 1936, and cited by Ramos, p. 123.

19. See Portillo, *op. cit.,* p. 123.

20. *Ibid.,* pp. 26–27.

21. Arniches' connection with the Generation of '98 has been mentioned most recently by Gáspar Gómez de la Serna, "Madrid y su gente: Arniches," in *ABC* (Madrid, April 17, 1963); José Bergamín, "Arniches o El teatro de verdad," in *Primer Acto,* No. 40 (Madrid, February, 1963), pp. 5–10; and José Monleón, "Arniches: La crisis de la restauración," in *Carlos Arniches: Teatro* (Madrid: Taurus, 1967), pp. 31–51.

22. Benavente and Valle-Inclán were born the same year as Arniches (1866). Unamuno was born two years earlier, Ganivet one year earlier, Baroja and Azorín six and seven years later, respectively.

23. An excellent synopsis of the impressions that Madrid produced in the minds of the major representatives of the Generation of '98 can be found in Pedro Laín Entralgo's *La generación del noventa y ocho* (Madrid: Espasa-Calpe, 1963), pp. 79–88.

24. *Ibid.,* p. 82.

25. The drama critic Gonzalo Torrente Ballester might disagree with this statement. In February of 1966 he was quoted as having said that "the most innocuous appearing plays of Arniches contain a bitter critical feeling which would ally him with the members of the Generation of '98, a feeling that is not expressed in concepts, after Benavente's manner, but rather in the selection of types and situations, in his way of conceiving them, in the development of conflicts and in their solution." See Juan Emilio Aragonés, "Costumbrismo y sainete trágico," in *La Estafeta Literaria,* No. 338 (Madrid, February 26, 1966), p. 6.

26. Arturo Berenguer Carísomo, *El teatro de Carlos Arniches* (Buenos Aires: Gráfico Argentino, 1937), p. 102.

27. Alfredo Marquerie, "Sobre la vida y la obra de don Carlos Arniches," in *Cuadernos de literatura contemporánea,* Nos. 9–10 (Madrid: Consejo Superior de Investigaciones Científicas, 1943), 249–55.

28. Marquerie. *Veinte años . . . ,* p. 55.

29. "Autorretrato," p. 10.

30. See *Diccionario de la lengua española,* 16th ed. (Madrid: Real Academia Española, 1939), p. 388.

31. See José Vega. *Ramón de la Cruz, el poeta de Madrid* (Madrid: Los libros del ayer y del mañana, 1945), p. 156; Nicolás González Ruiz, *La cultura española en los últimos veinte años: El teatro* (Madrid: Instituto de Cultura Hispánica, 1949), pp. 14–15.

32. José Bergamín, *op. cit.,* pp. 9–10.

33. Ramón Pérez de Ayala first disclosed his genuine interest in Arniches as a serious writer of dramatic literature in a personal letter to the playwright, dated August 4, 1916. See M. Cardenal de Iracheta, "Don Carlos Arniches al sesgo (Documentos del archivo de don Carlos Arniches)," in *Cuadernos de literatura contemporánea,* Nos. 9–10 (Madrid: Consejo Superior de Investigaciones Científicas, 1943), pp. 292–93.

34. Ramón Pérez de Ayala, *Las máscaras,* II (Madrid: Editorial Saturnino Calleja, 1919), p. 224.

35. A statement recorded by Federico Navas, *Las esfinges de Talía, o Encuesta sobre la crisis del teatro* (Real Monasterio de La Escorial, 1928), p. 11.

36. *Ibid.*

37. Berenguer Carísomo, *op. cit.,* p. 106.

38. See "Entrevista con Arniches," in *La Nación* (Buenos Aires, January 10, 1937).

39. From a review of Arniches' tragicomedy, *El solar de Mediacapa (Mediacapa's Lineage),* in *El Imparcial* (Madrid, December 22, 1928).

40. See Matilde Muñoz. *Teatro dramático en España* (Madrid: Tesoro, 1948), p. 311.

41. See Juan Emilio Aragonés, *op. cit.,* p. 7.

42. Pedro Salinas. *Literatura española siglo XX* (Mexico: Lucero, 1941), pp. 196–97.

43. Federico García Lorca, "Entrevistas y declaraciones," *Obras Completas,* VI (Madrid: Aguilar), p. 1775.

Chapter Two

1. See *Diccionario de autoridades,* Facsimile ed. of 1732, II (Madrid: Biblioteca Románica Hispánica, Gredos, 1964), p. 519.

2. Edwin Honig, "On the Interludes of Cervantes," in *Miguel de Cervantes: Interludes* (New York: The New American Library, 1964), pp. ix-x.

3. Charles V. Aubrun affirms that the interludes often served, along with the play's prologue *(loa)* and its mumming dance *(mojiganga),* to interfere with comic illusion, thus hindering "the public's complete involvement." See *La comedia española (1600–1680)* (Madrid: Taurus, 1968), pp. 20–22.

4. Prologue to Luis Quiñones de Benavente's *Jocoseria,* ed. by Cayetano Rosell (Madrid: Libros de antaño, 1872), I, xix.

5. See Eugenio Asensio's fine monograph, *Itinerario del entremés: Desde Lope de Rueda a Quiñones de Benavente* (Madrid: Biblioteca Románica Hispánica, Gredos, 1965), pp. 18–24.

6. *Ibid.,* p. 40.

7. Cf. Emiliano Díez-Echarri and José María Roca Franquesa, *Historia de la literatura española e hispanoamericana,* 2nd ed. (Madrid: Aguilar), pp. 275–76.

8. George Tyler Northup, *The Spanish Farces of the 16th, 17th, and 18th Centuries* (Boston: D.C. Heath & Co., 1922), p. ix.

9. William Shaffer Jack, *The Early Entremés in Spain: The Rise of a Dramatic Form* (Philadelphia: Publications of the University of Pennsylvania, Series in Romance Languages and Literature No. 8, 1923), p. 65.

10. Two good studies dealing with this and other related common types are J. P. Wickersham Crawford's "The Braggart Soldier and the *Rufián* in the Spanish Drama of the 16th Century," in *Romanic Review,* II, 1911; and Raymond Leonard Grismer's *The Influence of Plautus in Spain Before Lope de Vega* (New York: Hispanic Institute, 1944).

11. Honig, *op. cit.,* pp. xxiii–xxiv.

12. Miguel Romera Navarro lists the primary character types in Lope de Rueda as being "the fool, the cowardly ruffian, the cursing lackey, the dumb but good-natured Negress, the Morisco with his unintelligible jargon, the pedantic quack, the crafty peasant, the gypsy of cunning skills, the ridiculous, ill-humored and impertinent old man." See his *Historia de la literatura española* (Boston: D.C. Heath & Co., 1928), p. 199.

13. Asensio, *op. cit.,* p. 58.

14. Honig, p. ix.

15. *Ibid.,* p. xx.

16. Paolo Savi López. *Cervantes.* Trans. from the Italian by Antonio G. Solalinde (Madrid: Calleja, 1917) and quoted by Díez-Echarri, *op. cit.,* p. 353.

17. Angel del Río. *Historia de la literatura española,* Revised Edition, I (New York: Holt, Rinehart and Winston, 1963), p. 297.

18. Honig, p. xi.

19. An excellent critical study on Quiñones de Benavente's contributions to this genre is found in Hannah E. Bergman's *Luis Quiñones de Benavente y sus entremeses* (Madrid: Editorial Castalia, 1965). At this writing Professor Bergman is completing a volume on Quiñones as part of Twayne's World Authors Series.

20. Cf. G.T. Northup, *op. cit.,* p. xxv.

21. Cf. Luis Astrana Marín. "Entremeses," in *Cervantinas y otros ensayos* (Madrid: Afrodisio Aguado, 1944), p. 189.

22. Emilio Cotarelo y Mori, in a modest effort to classify Quiñones de

Benavente's diverse writings for the stage, identifies 142 completely original works. See his *Colección de entremeses, bailes, jácaras y mojigangas desde fines del siglo XVI a mediados del XVIII* (Madrid: Nueva Biblioteca de Autores Españoles, XVIII, 1911).

23. Asensio, p. 124.

24. See, for instance, Emilio Cotarelo y Mori's series of articles entitled "Historia de la zarzuela" in *Boletín de la Real Academia Española* (Madrid, 1928–1934); and Federico Carlos Sainz de Robles, *Diccionario de la literatura,* I (Madrid: Aguilar, 1965), pp. 1211–16.

25. Among the dramatists who participated in this musical renaissance for the stage were Lope de Vega, Tirso de Molina, Vélez de Guevara, Ruiz de Alarcón, Agustín Moreto, Pérez de Montalbán, and Calderón de la Barca.

26. On three occasions, in fact, Arniches was completely unconventional with his use of the term "zarzuela." He assigned the name to one of his two-act farces and to two of his three-act musical comedies, any one of which could just as well have been designated a musical sainete, juguete, humorada, or comedia.

27. See Juan Corominas, *Diccionario crítico y etimológico de la lengua castellana,* IV (Madrid: Gredos, 1957), pp. 118–19.

28. Vicente Ramos, *Vida y teatro de Carlos Arniches* (Madrid: Alfaguara, 1966), pp. 63–64.

29. C. E. Kany, *Five Sainetes of Ramón de la Cruz* (Boston: Ginn and Company, 1926), p. xii.

30. See José Subirá, *Historia de la música teatral en España* (Barcelona: Editorial Labor, 1945), p. 143.

31. Northup, *op. cit.,* p. xxx.

32. Kany, p. xiii.

33. William Flint Thrall and Allison Hibbard, *A Handbook to Literature* (New York: Garden City, 1936), p. 197.

34. See Bartholow V. Crawford, "High Comedy in Terms of Restoration Practice," in *Philological Quarterly,* VIII (1929), p. 343.

35. Up to now the best biography and documented analysis of his writings are found in Emilio Cotarelo y Mori's monograph, *Don Ramón de la Cruz y sus obras* (Madrid: José Perales y Martínez, 1899). At this writing Professor John A. Moore has in press a volume on Cruz as part of Twayne's World Authors Series.

36. Kany, pp. xxi–xxii.

37. See Jack Horace Parker, *Breve historia del teatro español* (Mexico: Andrea, 1957), p. 99.

38. See the unsigned interview recorded under the caption "Está en Buenos Aires Carlos Arniches," in *La Nación* (Buenos Aires, January 10, 1937).

39. See Arthur Hamilton, "A Study of Spanish Manners 1750–1800

From the Plays of Ramón de la Cruz," in *University of Illinois Studies in Language and Literature,* Vol. XI, No. 3 (Urbana, 1926), p. 10.

40. Alfredo Marquerie, *Alfonso Paso y su teatro* (Madrid: Escelicer, 1960), pp. 75–76.

41. See Marciano Zurita, *Historia del género chico* (Madrid: Prensa Popular, 1920), p. 37.

42. José Martínez Ruiz (Azorín). *Los Quinteros, y otras páginas* (Madrid: R. Caro Raggio, 1925), p. 24.

43. Arniches appears to have been drawn to his birthplace on the Mediterranean with particular force during the years 1901–1902, at which time he centered four of his one-act musical plays in Andalusia. *Doloretes* takes place in a small Alicante village, *La divisa (The Emblem)* in a Valencian town, *Andalusian Gazpacho* and *A Handful of Roses* both in small villages of Andalusia.

44. See Zurita, *op. cit.* and Deleito y Piñuela's more complete study, *Origen y apogeo del "Género chico"* (Madrid: Revista de Occidente, 1949).

45. Deleito y Piñuela, p. xi.

46. Zurita, p. 11.

47. Rubén Darío, Preface to *Cantos de vida y esperanza* (Buenos Aires: Espasa Calpe, 1940), p. 20.

48. Quoted by Federico Carlos Sainz de Robles in his *Ensayos de un diccionario de la literatura,* I, 3rd ed. (Madrid: Aguilar, 1965), p. 542.

49. The glorious era of the *género chico* is both a product of and an influence upon a determined period of Spanish history, and as such suggests multiple possibilities for extensive investigation. The subject is merely hinted at by Fernando Vela, "El género chico," in *Revista de Occidente,* X (Madrid, 1965), pp. 364–69.

Chapter Three

1. Listed alphabetically with the number of plays they coauthored with Arniches provided in parentheses, his collaborators include the following writers: Joaquín Abati (13), Juan Aguilar Catena (1), Ramón Asensio Mas (3), R. Calleja (1), Gonzalo Cantó (11), Antonio Casero (1), Sinesio Delgado (3), Antonio Estremera (11), Carlos Fernández Shaw (3), Enrique García Álvarez (25), Pedro García Marín (2), José Jackson Veyán (7), Manuel Labra (2), José López Silva (4), Celso Lucio (24), José de Lucio (3), Julio Pardo (1), Antonio Paso (5), Félix Quintana (1), Juan G. Renovales (1), Emilio Sáez (1), Alfredo Trigueros Candel (1).

2. See his "Autorretrato," in *Teatro completo,* III (Madrid: Aguilar, 1948), p. 10.

3. *Ibid.*

4. Gonzalo Torrente Ballester, "El género chico," in *Primer Acto,* No. 40 (Madrid, February, 1963), p. 4.

5. "El género chico," in *Revista de Occidente,* X (Madrid: 1965), p. 364.

6. Vicente Ramos, *Vida y teatro de Carlos Arniches* (Madrid: Alfaguara, 1966), p. 62.

7. The *astracán* is a farcical composition in which dialogue is central to the comic situation. Its singular feature is the deliberate reduction of verisimilitude. Puns, jests, and plays on words are constantly used, contrived solely to evoke laughter. The original *astracán* is devoid of serious intention. It depends entirely upon repartee and dislocated speech for its effect, rather than character involvement or a clever plot line. In the hands of García Álvarez it is totally innocuous, with little political or social parody. It is likewise far removed from recognizable topics of the day, excepting an obvious exploitation of the comic possibilities in everyday speech.

8. Marquerie, "Sobre la vida y la obra de don Carlos Arniches," in *Cuadernos de literatura contemporánea,* Nos. 9–10 (Madrid, 1943), p. 249.

9. José Casado, *Las pirámides de sal: Enrique García Álvarez, verdadero libro de risa* (Madrid, 1919), pp. 160–61.

10. Mihura, *Obras completas* (Barcelona: AHR, 1962), p. 25.

11. Enrique Jardiel Poncela, *Tres comedias con un solo ensayo* (Madrid: Biblioteca Nueva, 1943), p. 25.

12. Quoted by Angel Laborda in *ABC* (Madrid, December 4, 1968), p. 91.

13. Mariano Zurita. *Historia del género chico* (Madrid: Prensa Popular, 1920), p. 106.

14. *Ibid.,* p. 113.

15. Ramos, *op. cit.,* p. 129.

16. The drama critic González Ruiz terms the quarter century of the *astracán*'s currency (1912–1936) a time of "frenzy of exaggeration and of nonsense." See his article, "El teatro de humor del siglo XX hasta Jardiel Poncela," in J. Rof Carballo *et al., El teatro de humor en España* (Madrid: Editora Nacional, 1966), p. 39.

17. Angel Valbuena Prat, *Historia del teatro español* (Barcelona: Noguer, 1956), p. 63.

18. Information conveyed in a personal interview with Miguel Mihura in Madrid, June 9, 1967.

19. Mihura, *op. cit.,* p. 25.

20. Arturo Berenguer Carísomo, *El teatro de Carlos Arniches* (Buenos Aires: Gráfico Argentino, 1937), p. 35.

21. Gonzalo Torrente Ballester, *Panorama de la literatura española contemporánea,* 1st ed. (Madrid: Guadarrama, 1956), p. 144.

22. Ramos, p. 106.

23. The "new appellation" under which the *pícaro* appears in the *género chico* may vary from *cesante* (a dismissed or retired public officer), to *sablista* (a sponger), to *chulo* (a low-class rascal). See Ruiz Morcuende's "Introducción" to Castillo Solorzano's *La garduña de Sevilla y anzvelo de las bolsas* (Madrid: Edición de "La Lectura," Clásicos Castellanos No. 42, 1922), xxix.

24. José Bergamín. "Reencuentro con Arniches, o El teatro de verdad," in *Carlos Arniches: Teatro,* ed. by José Monleón (Madrid: Taurus, 1967), p. 24.

25. Berenguer, p. 84.

26. Cf. José Casado, *op. cit.,* pp. 164 and 180.

27. Enrique Chicote, *Cuando Fernando VII gastaba paletó* (Madrid: Reus, 1952), p. 30.

28. Melchor Fernández Almagro, "Prólogo" to his edition of *Teatro escogido de Carlos Arniches,* IV (Madrid: Estampa, 1932), p. 10.

29. Arniches' leading composers, in addition to José Serrano, were R. Calleja, Ruperto Chapí, Tomás López Torregrosa, and Joaquín Valverde Sanjuán. One hundred of his plays include musical scores.

30. Zurita, p. 114.

31. Ramos, p. 109.

Chapter Four

1. Marciano Zurita, *Historia del género chico* (Madrid: Prensa Popular, 1920), p. 65.

2. Salinas, *Literatura española siglo XX* (Mexico: Séneca, 1941), pp. 191–92.

3. A public manifestation of disapproval, even hostile dissent, toward a work for the legitimate stage, has never been an unusual phenomenon among Spanish playgoers. Since at least as far back as Lope de Vega one can find instances of near-riotous conduct on the part of professional hecklers, called *reventadores.* Fearing this kind of imposed failure, Arniches often suffered agony on the nights of his premières.

4. The final scenes of Arniches' *Isidra's Saint* and *Saint Anthony's Festival* bring to mind Goya's canvas oils entitled "El columpio" ("The Swing") and "La Ermita de San Isidro el día de la fiesta" ("San Isidro's Chapel on Festival Day"). The opening scene of *El amigo Melquíades (Friend Melquíades)* recalls Goya's "La merienda a orillas del Manzanares" ("Picnic on the Banks of the Manzanares"). In 1918 Arniches wrote of the enduring qualities of the Madrilenean nature and thus allied his work with that of Goya's: "Over the years the people of Madrid have been able to modify their apparel, their aesthetic appearance; but nothing more. The soul of this people, the very soul immortalized by both Francisco de Goya and Ramón de la Cruz remains unalterable in its essence." See his Prologue to *El agua del Manzanares (The Waters of the Manzanares)* in *Obras completas,* ed. by Portillo, II (Madrid: Aguilar, 1948), p. 331.

5. E. Estévez Ortega, "Carlos Arniches," in *Nuevo Mundo* (Madrid, January 10, 1930), p. 4.

6. Salinas, p. 193.

7. Cf. Estévez Ortega, *op. cit.,* p. 4.

8. Arturo Berenguer Carísomo, *El teatro de Carlos Arniches* (Buenos Aires: Gráfico Argentino, 1937), pp. 66–67.

9. *Ibid.,* p. 68.

10. Vicente Ramos. *Vida y teatro de Carlos Arniches* (Madrid: Alfaguara, 1966), p. 62.

11. *Obras completas,* IV, p. 1009.

12. *Ibid.,* II, p. 331.

13. José Monleón, "Arniches: La crisis de la restauración," in *Carlos Arniches: Teatro,* ed. by Monleón (Madrid: Taurus, 1967), p. 49.

14. The quotation is from Arniches, *Obras completas, IV,* 1066.

15. *Ibid.*

16. *The Paupers,* for instance, which conveys the colorful language of the world of beggars and thieves, is not without influence on the first act of *The Forlorn Girl,* a three-act play about life in the Madrid underworld.

17. We venture this judgment cognizant of the historical fact that the theater climate of the era exacted an abandonment of the *género chico* in favor of more extensive plays. Arniches, of course, followed the currents of his day. And while he did revitalize the nature of the *género grande* with his tragicomedies and grotesque tragedies, there yet remains the debatable issue as to whether or not many of his other three-act plays, designated variously as sainetes, comedies, juguetes, farces, and even one zarzuela of that length, did in fact demonstrate a substantial improvement over the previous legitimate sainetes of realistic content.

18. Such statements in the state-controlled Spanish press are frequent and are usually intended as a warning to parents of young theatergoers. In Arniches' case, however, we suspect the criticism is less an impugnment for his having developed a topic about immorality, as it is a cry of dismay to find him abandoning the colorful and innocuous realm of *costumbrismo.* Many veterans of the *género chico* found it difficult to comprehend that in his last twenty years, Arniches had graduated to a more serious sphere of dramatic expression and was no longer simply an exponent of the folk sainete.

19. Cf. Ramos, p. 206.

20. Monleón, *op. cit.,* p. 43.

21. See, in this connection, the essay by Francisco García Pavón, "Arniches, autor casi comprometido," in Monleon, *op. cit.,* pp. 52–55.

Chapter Five

1. Julio Cejador y Frauca, *Historia de la lengua y literatura castellana,* X (Madrid: Tip. de la "Revista de arch., bibl. y museos," 1919), p. 126.

2. See, for instance, statements by José de Larcena in *El Imparcial* (Madrid), and Andrenio in *La Epoca* (Madrid), both reviews appearing February 14, 1920.

3. Arniches was a strong admirer of the Crown. He dedicated *The Bosses* "To His Majesty the King, Don Alfonso XIII" stating that the play was meant to depict "a bitter and living reality of Spanish political customs, expressed sincerely and nobly." See his preface to *The Bosses,* written March 10, 1920.

4. The melodrama *La sobrina del cura (The Priest's Niece)* is an earlier play resembling the conflict of *The Bosses,* but it lacks the clear political orientation of the rural farce. The antagonist, Señor Galo, is similar to the despotic mayor Acisclo of *The Bosses* in that he assumes special privileges because of his influence and money. A battle ensues between his power and the unsullied dignity of a humble priest.

5. See "Carlos Arniches: Costumbrismo y sainete trágico," in *La Estafeta Literaria,* No. 338 (Madrid, February 26, 1966), pp. 6–8.

6. José Monleón, ed. "Arniches: La crisis de la restauración," in *Carlos Arniches: Teatro* (Madrid: Taurus, 1967), p. 38.

7. Gregorio Marañón. "Sobre Arniches y el género chico," *La Nación* (Buenos Aires, May, 1949).

8. Ramón Pérez de Ayala. *Las máscaras,* II (Madrid: Editorial Saturnino Calleja, 1919), p. 226.

Chapter Six

1. Ramón Pérez de Ayala, *Las máscaras,* II (Madrid: Editorial Saturnino Calleja, 1919), pp. 223–52.

2. Teodoro Lipps. *Los fundamentos de la estética* (Madrid: Jorro, 1923), p. 563.

3. Melchor Fernández Almagro. "Prólogo" to *Teatro escogido de Carlos Arniches,* IV (Madrid: Estampa, 1932), p. 10.

4. Salinas, *Literatura española siglo XX* (Mexico: Lucero, 1941), pp. 185–97.

5. Ramos, *Vida y teatro de Carlos Arniches* (Madrid: Alfaguara, 1966), pp. 158 and 163.

6. See E. M. del Portillo's prologue, "Arniches y el estilo," in *Teatro completo,* ed. by Portillo, IV (Madrid: Aguilar, 1948), 13; and Ayala, *op. cit.,* p. 236.

7. Melchor Fernández Almagro, *En torno al '98: política y literatura* (Madrid: Jordan, 1948), p. 224. Fernández Almagro errs further in attributing Andreyev's play to Chekhov.

8. Luis Calvo, "Arniches," in *ABC* (Madrid, April 16, 1946).

9. Ramos, *op. cit.,* pp. 227–28.

10. Salinas, *op. cit.,* p. 196.
    Ramos, pp. 243–44.

Chapter Eight

1. Quoted by Julio Mathias, "Lo arnichesco: de la frase a la situación," in *La Estafeta Literaria,* No. 338 (Madrid, February 26, 1966), p. 8.
2. Domingo Pérez Minik. *Teatro europeo contemporáneo: Su libertad y compromisos* (Madrid: Guadarrama, 1961), p. 301.

Selected Bibliography

Bibliographies

JULIÁ MARTÍNEZ, EDUARDO. "Ante la obra de don Carlos Arniches, un siglo muere y otro nace," in *Idealidad* (Alicante), January, 1964, No. 71; Concluded in February, 1964, No. 72. A partial but fairly accurate listing of Arniches' plays.

LENTZEN, MANFRED. *Carlos Arniches: Vom "género chico" zur "tragedia grotesca"* (Geneva: Droz, 1966), pp. 208–18. A thorough, completely documented bibliography.

PORTILLO, EDUARDO MARÍA DEL. *Carlos Arniches: Teatro completo* (Madrid: Aguilar, 1948), IV, pp. 1097–1102. Attributes 167 titles to Arniches. The list of coauthored works contains a few errors.

RAMOS, VICENTE. *Vida y teatro de Carlos Arniches* (Madrid: Alfaguara, 1966), pp. 303–20. Lists 172 plays accurately.

ROMO ARREGUI, JOSEFINA. "Carlos Arniches, Bibliografía," in *Cuadernos de literatura contemporánea* (Madrid: Consejo Superior de Investigaciones Científicas, 1943), Nos. 9–10, pp. 299–307. First attempt to compile a bibliography of play editions. Omits over thirty titles and contains several errors.

PRIMARY SOURCES

The reader may turn to the Appendix for a list of Arniches' works, arranged chronologically and briefly annotated.

1. Selected Editions and Anthologies

García Rico y Cía. *Colección de comedias españolas de los siglos XIX y XX* (Madrid: Miscellaneous publishers, 1800–1941). Nos. 202–244 are plays by Arniches in collaboration with other playwrights.

Teatro escogido (Madrid: Estampa, 1932) 4 vols. This collection contains twelve plays, with prologues written by José Carner (Vol. 1), Ramón Pérez de Ayala (Vol. 2), A. Hernández Catá (Vol. 3), and Melchor Fernández Almagro (Vol. 4).

Teatro completo. Ed. by Eduardo María del Portillo (Madrid: Aguilar, 1948) 4 vols. Includes no coauthored plays.

La pareja científica y otros ensayos (Salamanca: Biblioteca Anaya, 1964) No. 49. Contains three "rapid sainetes" and an introduction by José Montero Padilla.

Teatro. Ed. by José Monleón (Madrid: Taurus, 1967). An outstanding critical anthology that includes *La señorita de Trevélez, La heroica*

villa, and *Los milagros del jornal.*
El santo de la Isidra. El amigo Melquiades. Los caciques. A paperback
edition (Madrid: Alianza Editorial, 1969).

SECONDARY SOURCES

The reader who is interested in single articles or reviews from periodicals
and journals, as well as general literary histories, is encouraged to consult
the bibliographies of secondary sources published by Lentzen and Ramos
in their respective books. The following list includes only selected titles
of books, monographs, theses, and special issues devoted to Arniches or to
the development of the *género chico.*

BERENGUER CARÍSOMO, ARTURO. *El teatro de Carlos Arniches* (Buenos Aires:
Gráfico Argentino, 1937). The first bibliographical and critical study
on Arniches, written to celebrate the playwright's inauguration into
the Ateneo Iberoamericano. Thoughtful comments on the highlights
of his theater.
CHICOTE, ENRIQUE. *Cuando Fernando VII gastaba paletó* (Madrid: Reus,
1952). An interesting series of personal recollections and anecdotes.
CONIS, JAMES NORMAN. "The Grotesque Tragedies of Carlos Arniches
y Barrera" (University of Virginia, 1965). An unpublished doctoral
thesis which explores the nature of the grotesque in six major plays.
Cuadernos de literatura contemporánea. Nos. 9–10 (Madrid: Consejo
Superior de Investigaciones Científicas, 1943), 249–307. An issue
of special tribute to Arniches written the year of his death.
DELEITO Y PIÑUELA, JOSÉ. *Estampas del Madrid teatral de fin de siglo* (Madrid:
Calleja, 1946). An excellent comprehensive view of the theater climate
during Arniches' early period.
————. *Origen y apogeo del "género chico"* (Madrid: Revista de Occidente,
1949). A penetrating exposition of theater activity in Madrid from
1868 to 1910.
LENTZEN, MANFRED. *Carlos Arniches: Vom "género chico" zur "tragedia
grotesca"* (Geneva: Droz, 1966). A published doctoral thesis from the
University of Cologne. A good general study on the evolution of
Arniches' theater, stressing themes, language, and character types.
MARQUERÍE, ALFREDO. *Veinte años de teatro en España* (Madrid: Editora
Nacional, 1959), pp. 49–59. A succinct résumé of the playwright's
major defects and accomplishments.
MONLEÓN, JOSÉ (ed.). *Carlos Arniches: Teatro* (Madrid: Taurus, 1967).
An excellent collection of essays on Arniches followed by the complete
texts of three plays.
PÉREZ DE AYALA, RAMÓN. *Las máscaras: ensayos de crítica teatral,* I (Madrid:
Saturnino Calleja, 1919), pp. 223–52. A too personal judgment on
major writers, including an encomium on Arniches in two essays.

Primer Acto, No. 40 (Madrid, February, 1963), pp. 2–47. Issue devoted
to Arniches, with critical articles and the complete text of *Los caciques.*

RAMOS, VICENTE. *Vida y teatro de Carlos Arniches* (Madrid: Alfaguara,
1966). An excellent biography, historically oriented with sound critical
insight.

SECO, MANUEL. *Arniches y el habla de Madrid* (Madrid: Alfaguara, 1970).
A penetrating study of Arniches' use of the Madrilenean vernacular.
Contains a lengthy lexicon of popular words and expressions and the
text of *Los tiros,* a newly discovered *sainete rápido* written in 1915.

TRINIDAD, FRANCISCO. *A Study of Madrid's Dialect in Arniches' Plays*
(University of California, Los Angeles, 1969). Doctoral thesis. A
tripartite approach to the peculiarities of language in Arniches' Madrid
writings: phonetic, morphological, and lexicographic features.

VALENCIA, ANTONIO (ed.). *El género chico (Antología de textos completos)*
(Madrid: Taurus, 1962). A well-conceived selection of the fifteen best
plays of the *género chico,* with introductory notes.

ZURITA, MARCIANO. *Historia del género chico* (Madrid: Prensa Popular,
1920). A treatise of anecdotes and history that situates Arniches in his
time among his contemporaries.

APPENDIX

Plays by Carlos Arniches

The plays are listed in chronological order according to the date of their première. When the city is not mentioned, the première took place in Madrid.

1. *Publishing House (Casa Editorial);* one act; February 9, 1888. Written in collaboration with Gonzalo Cantó. Music by Rafael Taboada. A musical satire on nineteenth-century Spanish literature.
2. *The Naked Truth (La verdad desnuda);* one act; July 7, 1888. Written in collaboration with Gonzalo Cantó. Music by Apolinar Brull. A social satire that personifies law, justice, and public order.
3. *Manias (Las manías);* one act; November 15, 1888. Written in collaboration with Gonzalo Cantó. Music by Fernández Caballero. A landlady's troubles with the indigence of her boarders. A trivial musical revue.
4. *Orthography (Ortografía);* one act; December 31, 1888. Written in collaboration with Gonzalo Cantó. Music by Ruperto Chapí. A musical parade of personified letters and signs satirizing language, politics, and social conventions.
5. *St. Elmo's Fire (El fuego de San Telmo);* one act; October 26, 1889. Written in collaboration with Gonzalo Cantó. Music by Apolinar Brull. Comic sainete of light social satire.
6. *National Panorama (Panorama nacional);* one act; November 8, 1889. Written in collaboration with Celso Lucio. Music by Apolinar Brull. Musical revue contrasting characters, customs, and costumes of the past with those of the present time, satirizing the latter.
7. *Secret Society (Sociedad secreta);* one act; December 17, 1889. Written in collaboration with Sinesio Delgado, Celso Lucio, and Fernández Manzano. Music by Apolinar Brull. Comic-lyric revue.
8. *The Garrets (Las guardillas);* one act; January 10, 1890. Written in collaboration with Gonzalo Cantó. Mistaken identities between two pretenders for a girl's hand. A good sainete in a tenement apartment setting.
9. *Calderón;* one act; November 10, 1890. Written in collaboration with Celso Lucio. Music by Manuel Nieto. Two husbands suspect their wives of infidelity.

10. *Our Wife (Nuestra señora);* one act; November 25, 1890. Arniches' first play by his own hand. The misadventures of a married woman masquerading as the wife of another married man.

11. *The Legend of the Monk (La leyenda del monje);* one act; December 6, 1890. Written in collaboration with Gonzalo Cantó. Music by Ruperto Chapí. Humorous zarzuela in which a young stranger is mistaken for the ghost of a penitent monk.

12. *Victory! (¡Victoria!);* one act; August 19, 1891. Written in collaboration with Manuel Labra. Music by Tomás López Torregrosa. A provincial father's woes as he tries to locate his daughter and her husband in a Madrid hotel.

13. *Independent Candidate (Candidato independiente);* one act; November 10, 1891. Written in collaboration with Gonzalo Cantó. Sainete of social satire.

14. *The Kidnappers (Los secuestradores);* one act; February 3, 1892. Written in collaboration with Celso Lucio. Music by Manuel Nieto. A mild-mannered school teacher mistaken for a ruthless bandit. Sainete in small-town setting.

15. *The Ghosts (Los aparecidos);* one act; February 23, 1892. Written in collaboration with Celso Lucio. Music by Fernández Caballero. A comic actor in disguise as the statue from Zorrilla's *Tenorio* terrifies an entire town. A zany rural zarzuela.

16. *The Stroking of the Bell (Las campanadas);* one act; May 13, 1892. Written in collaboration with Gonzalo Cantó. Music by Ruperto Chapí. A double elopement causes a church bell to chime the alarm to superstitious townsfolk.

17. *The Mostenses (Los Mostenses);* three acts; December 6, 1892. Written in collaboration with Gonzalo Cantó and Celso Lucio. Music by Ruperto Chapí. A comic zarzuela about small-town antics and feuds.

18. *Open Road (Vía libre);* one act; April 25, 1893. Written in collaboration with Gonzalo Cantó and Celso Lucio. Music by Ruperto Chapí. The changes that occur with the arrival of the first train to a small town.

19. *The Ragamuffins (Los descamisados);* one act; October 31, 1893. Written in collaboration with José López Silva. Music by Federico Chueca. Obsessed with political zeal, a foolish carpenter declares himself a candidate for councilman.

20. *The Right Arm (El brazo derecho);* one act; November 11, 1893. Written in collaboration with Celso Lucio and Joaquín Abati. A comedy of errors.

21. *The Decoy (El reclamo);* one act; November 25, 1893. Written in collaboration with Celso Lucio. Music by Ruperto Chapí. A small love conflict with amusing play on words.

22. *The Puritans (Los puritanos)*; one act; March 31, 1894. Written in collaboration with Celso Lucio. Music by J. Valverde and Tomás López Torregrosa. A renegade's hunger inspires wily acts to eat gratis in a restaurant. A hilarious lyrical farce.
23. *The Left Foot (El pie izquierdo)*; one act; June 21, 1894. Written in collaboration with Celso Lucio. A comic sequel to *The Right Arm*.
24. *The Poppies (Las amapolas)*; one act; June 21, 1894. Written in collaboration with Celso Lucio. Music by Tomás López Torregrosa. A lively zarzuela.
25. *Tabardillo*; one act; March 14, 1895. Written in collaboration with Celso Lucio. Music by Tomás López Torregrosa. A coward's pretense as a fearless warrior leads to heroism during the Spanish uprising of 1808.
26. *The First Corporal (El cabo primero)*; one act; May 24, 1895. Written in collaboration with Celso Lucio. Music by Fernández Caballero. A zarzuela based on the rivalry of soldiers quartered in a small town.
27. *The Other World (El otro mundo)*; one act; October 12, 1895. Written in collaboration with Joaquín Abati. A comic farce about the supernatural.
28. *The Princely Heir (El príncipe heredero)*; two acts; January 9, 1896. Written in collaboration with Celso Lucio. Music by Manuel Nieto, Apolinar Brull, and Tomás López Torregrosa. The misadventures of a Spanish tribal prince in Africa.
29. *The Mail Car (El coche correo)*; one act; April 4, 1896. Written in collaboration with José López Silva. Music by Federico Chueca. Unsuccessful sainete about a love mix-up.
30. *Evil Tongues (Las malas lenguas)*; one act; July 4, 1896. Written in collaboration with Celso Lucio. Music by Jerónimo Jiménez. A community infected by the gossip of one thoughtless individual.
31. *The Activity Boss (El jefe del movimiento)*; one act; July 31, 1896. Written in collaboration with Manuel Labra. Music by Tomás López Torregrosa. Pretended bomb scares and practical jokes surround a theme of anarchism.
32. *The Bandits (Los bandidos)*; one act; December 24, 1896. Written in collaboration with Celso Lucio. Music by Tomás López Torregrosa. A harmless and fearful Italian unwittingly finds himself in the company of ruthless bandits.
33. *The Trumpet Band (La banda de trompetas)*; one act; December 24, 1896. Music by Tomás López Torregrosa. First zarzuela without coauthorship. Military pranks among amiable villagers.
34. *The Rabbits (Los conejos)*; one act; March 27, 1897. Written in collaboration with Celso Lucio. False pretenses by members of an impoverished noble family alienate a prospective wealthy suitor.

35. *Plan of Attack (Plan de ataque);* one act; April 7, 1897. Written in collaboration with Celso Lucio and Julio Pardo. Music by Audran and Vidal Llimona. Semiserious war skirmishes rendered with shallow humor.

36. *Rainbow (Arco iris);* one act; May 14, 1897. Written in collaboration with Celso Lucio and Enrique García Álvarez. Music by J. Valverde and Tomás López Torregrosa. First work of collaboration with García Álvarez.

37. *Gratuities (Los camarones);* one act; December 4, 1897. Written in collaboration with Celso Lucio. Music by J. Valverde and Tomás López Torregrosa. A bogus doctor endeavors to dissolve a marriage of convenience.

38. *The Soldiers in Yellow (La guardia amarilla);* one act; December 31, 1897. Written in collaboration with Celso Lucio. Music by Jerónimo Jiménez. A courtship by courier across sixteenth-century battle lines.

39. *Isidra's Saint (El santo de la Isidra);* one act; February 19, 1898. Music by Tomás López Torregrosa. Charming folk sainete based on May 15 San Isidro Festival. A cowardly bully in conflict with a timid but chivalrous hero. Arniches' most celebrated sainete.

40. *St. Anthony's Festival (La fiesta de San Antón);* one act; November 24, 1898. Music by Tomás López Torregrosa. Two girls vie for attention of one man amid the gaiety of a January 17 folk festival. An inferior sequel to *Isidra's Saint.*

41. *The Day of San Eugenio (El día de San Eugenio);* one act; 1899. Unpublished sainete about folk customs.

42. *Snapshots (Instantáneas);* one act; June 28, 1899. Written in collaboration with José López Silva. Music by Tomás López Torregrosa. A provincial photographer goes to Madrid in search of his runaway girlfriend.

43. *The Last Scamp (El último chulo);* one act; November 7, 1899. Written in collaboration with Celso Lucio. Music by Tomás López Torregrosa and J. Valverde. An outlandish exploitation of puns and linguistic games. Mediocre.

44. *God's Countenance (La cara de Dios);* three acts; November 28, 1899. Music by Ruperto Chapí. Melodramatic love conflict involving a woman unjustly spurned by her husband. Focus on popular folk festivities of Holy Week celebration.

45. *María de los Angeles;* one act; May 12, 1900. Written in collaboration with Celso Lucio. Music by Ruperto Chapí. Zarzuela accenting virtue and honesty.

46. *The Housebreaking (El escalo);* one act; 1900. Written in collaboration with Celso Lucio. Music by Amadeo Vives. Mistaken identities in a presumed robbery of a watchmaker's shop.

47. *A Cart of Melons (Sandías y melones);* one act; December 17, 1900. Music by Eladio Montero. A timorous lad jilts a poor girl to marry for money, then reverses his decision. Popular sainete.
48. *The Nineteenth Century (El siglo XIX);* one act; February 6, 1901. Written in collaboration with Sinesio Delgado and José López Silva. Music by Montesinos. Panoramic revue depicting customs of recent past.
49. *The Fellow From Alcalá (El tío de Alcalá):* one act; April 15, 1901. Music by Montesinos. A young lady's cleverness to avoid suitors results in an authentic romance. A flimsy comedietta.
50. *Doloretes;* one act; June 28, 1901. Music by Amado Vives and Manuel Quislant. An offended lover punishes his inconstant girlfriend. A forceful character and *costumbrista* study.
51. *The Whining Children (Los niños llorones);* one act; July 4, 1901. Written in collaboration with Enrique García Álvarez and Antonio Paso. Music by Tomás López Torregrosa, J. Valverde, and Tomás Barrera. A confusion of identities and a profusion of practical jokes during Carnival.
52. *Agrippina's Death (La muerte de Agripina);* one act; April 5, 1902. Written in collaboration with Enrique García Álvarez. Music by J. Valverde and Tomás López Torregrosa. Mediocre lyric farce of melodramatic appeal.
53. *The Emblem (La divisa);* one act; April 15, 1902. Music by Tomás López Torregrosa. A zarzuela of moral intent that damns envy as a cardinal sin.
54. *Andalusian Gazpacho (Gazpacho andaluz);* one act; April 30, 1902. Music by R. Calleja and V. Lleó. Lyrical comedy offering good advice for a happy marriage.
55. *San Juan de Luz;* one act; July 9, 1902. Written in collaboration with José Jackson Veyán. Music by J. Valverde and Tomás López Torregrosa. Vacation capers at an oceanside resort on the French border.
56. *A Handful of Roses (El puñao de rosas);* one act; October 30, 1902. Written in collaboration with Ramón Asensio Mas. Music by Ruperto Chapí. Delightful zarzuela about Andalusian customs.
57. *The Urchins (Los granujas);* one act; November 8, 1902. Written in collaboration with José Jackson Veyán. Music by J. Valverde and Tomás López Torregrosa. Zarzuela that centers on small-town mischiefmakers.
58. *The Castaway's Song (La canción del náufrago);* three acts; February 18, 1903. Written in collaboration with Carlos Fernández Shaw. Music by Morera. Lyrical drama stressing music over an insubstantial plot.

59. *Terrible Pérez (El terrible Pérez)*; one act; May 1, 1903. Written in collaboration with Enrique García Álvarez. Music by Tomás López Torregrosa and J. Valverde. A laughable would-be Don Juan overestimates his seductive charms.

60. *Bright and Ruddy (Colorín, colorao)*; one act; July 11, 1903. Written in collaboration with José Jackson Veyán. Music by Tomás López Torregrosa and J. Valverde. A musical tale of fantasy for children of all ages.

61. *The Schoolboys (Los chicos de la escuela)*; one act; December 22, 1903. Written in collaboration with José Jackson Veyán. Music by Tomás López Torregrosa and J. Valverde. Zarzuela about the problems of growing up.

62. *Vile Suspicions (Los pícaros celos)*; one act; June 22, 1904. Written in collaboration with Carlos Fernández Shaw. Music by Jerónimo Jiménez. Comedy dealing with jealousy, both unfounded and well grounded. Good folk sainete set in Madrid's slums.

63. *Poor Valbuena (El pobre Valbuena)*; one act; July 1, 1904. Written in collaboration with Enrique García Álvarez. Music by J. Valverde and Tomás López Torregrosa. A versatile rascal feigns epilepsy to attract female attention.

64. *The Children's Paradise (El paraíso de los niños)*; one act; December 28, 1904. Written in collaboration with Sinesio Delgado. Music by J. Valverde. A charming zarzuela of fantasy written for children.

65. *The Stars (Las estrellas)*; one act; December 30, 1904. Music by Valverde and José Serrano. A father's lofty but unrealistic plans nearly destroys his home. An outstanding lyrical sainete.

66. *The Bullies (Los guapos)*; one act; April 22, 1905. Written in collaboration with José Jackson Veyán. Music by Jerónimo Jiménez. Mischief repaid in kind. An unsuccessful zarzuela.

67. *The Five-Cent Coin (El perro chico)*; one act; May 5, 1905. Written in collaboration with Enrique García Álvarez. Music by José Serrano and J. Valverde. Humorous pranks among lower-class *chulos* of Madrid.

68. *Dolores' Window (La reja de la Dolores)*; one act; September 26, 1905. Written in collaboration with Enrique García Álvarez. Music by José Serrano and J. Valverde. Comic zarzuela around small love conflict.

69. *Deluded Cañizares (El iluso Cañizares)*; one act; December 22, 1905. Written in collaboration with Enrique García Álvarez. and Antonio Casero. Music by J. Valverde and R. Calleja. An inept and ignorant commoner becomes governor and bungles the post.

70. *Accursed Money (El maldito dinero)*; one act; May 8, 1906. Written in collaboration with Carlos Fernández Shaw. Music by Ruperto Chapí. Lyrical sainete stressing the woes of material gain.

71. *Shrewd Tejada (El pollo Tejada)*; one act; May 29, 1906. Written

in collaboration with Enrique García Álvarez. Music by J. Valverde and José Serrano. The absurd adventures of a lecherous old man.

72. *The Dark Affliction (La pena negra);* one act; October 30, 1906. Music by J. Valverde and Tomás López Torregrosa. A girl's impossible and silent love for her cousin, their economic strain, and parental disputation. A competent sainete.

73. *The Distinguished Sportsman (El distinguido "sportsman");* entremés; November 22, 1906. Written in collaboration with Enrique García Álvarez. Music by J. Valverde. A musical interlude that focuses on comic dialogue.

74. *Twelfth Night (La noche de Reyes);* one act; December 15, 1906. Music by José Serrano. A man's angry revenge is stilled by the spirit of Christmas and a small child's anticipation. Zarzuela on the sierra among shepherds.

75. *The Iron Age (La edad de hierro);* one act; March 30, 1907. Written in collaboration with Enrique García Álvarez and Ramón Asensio Mas. Music by García Álvarez and Hermoso. A love conflict erupts among a theater troupe on the eve of their major performance.

76. *The Serious People (La gente seria);* one act; April 25, 1907. Written in collaboration with Enrique García Álvarez. Music by José Serrano. Lyrical sainete that extols the importance of laughter.

77. *Crazy Luck (La suerte loca);* one act; June 19, 1907. Written in collaboration with Enrique García Álvarez. Music by J. Valverde and José Serrano. A streak of good fortune that knows no bounds.

78. *The Kindhearted Woman (Alma de Dios);* one act; December 17, 1907. Written in collaboration with Enrique García Álvarez. Music by José Serrano. A vilified orphan girl struggles to vindicate her honor. A sensitive, well-written melodrama.

79. *Weak Flesh (La carne flaca);* one act; March 21, 1908. Written in collaboration with José Jackson Veyán. Music by V. Lleó. Human weakness condoned when compensated for by salutary strength.

80. *The Ferret; Philip the Second (El hurón; Felipe Segundo);* two entremeses; May 9, 1908. Written in collaboration with Enrique García Álvarez. Music by Tomás López Torregrosa. Brief lyrical interludes for comic entertainment.

81. *The Battalion's Merriment (La alegría del batallón);* one act; March 11, 1909. Written in collaboration with Félix Quintana. Music by José Serrano. Humorous good times in the military.

82. *The Górritz Method (El método Górritz);* one act; June, 1909. Written in collaboration with Enrique García Álvarez. Music by V. Lleó. The misadventures of a typical *fresco* whose ingenious plan goes awry.

83. *My Dad (Mi papá);* three acts; January 26, 1910. Written in collaboration with Enrique García Álvarez. An old man assumes the role of father for his young friend in need of help.

84. *The First Conquest (La primera conquista);* entremés; March 12, 1910. Written in collaboration with Enrique García Álvarez. A laughable rustic encounters problems trying to woo young ladies in Madrid.

85. *The Street Boss (El amo de la calle);* one act; April 20, 1910. Written in collaboration with José López Silva. Music by Enrique García Álvarez and R. Calleja. A sainete fashioned around typical folkways on the city street.

86. *Smart and Shapely (Genio y figura);* three acts; November 16, 1910. Written in collaboration with Enrique García Álvarez, Antonio Paso, and Joaquín Abati. The love entanglements and disputes of a fancy-free family.

87. *The Trust of the Tenorios (El trust de los Tenorios);* one act; December 3, 1910. Written in collaboration with Enrique García Álvarez. Music by José Serrano. A weak farce about a frustrated Don Juan.

88. *The Nobel Prize (El Premio Nobel);* three acts; January 31, 1911. Written in collaboration with Joaquín Abati. A presumptuous druggist thirsts for glory. Patterned after André Mouézy-Éon and Eugène Joullot's play, *Le Major Ipeca* (1906).

89. *Little People (Gente menuda);* two acts; May 7, 1911. Written in collaboration with Enrique García Álvarez. Music by J. Valverde. Sainete about the nameless, forgotten people on Madrid's backstreets.

90. *The Happy Genre (El género alegre);* one act; September 7, 1911. Written in collaboration with Ramón Asensio Mas. Music by Penella and Enrique García Álvarez. A fantasy that vindicates the value of song and dance.

91. *Prince Casto (El príncipe Casto);* one act; February 14, 1912. Written in collaboration with Enrique García Álvarez. Music by J. Valverde. Comic zarzuela of little merit.

92. *Rascally Goya (El fresco de Goya);* one act; March 22, 1912. Written in collaboration with Enrique García Álvarez. Music by Antonio Domínguez and J. Valverde. A married man's extra-marital interests lead to his discovery and punishment.

93. *The Pons Quartet (El cuarteto Pons);* one act; April 19, 1912. Written in collaboration with Enrique García Álvarez. Music by V. Lleó. Zarzuela on the theme of musical entertainment.

94. *The Poor Little Girl (La pobre niña);* three acts; November 22, 1912. A girl's friends turn avaricious when she receives a modest fortune. First definite signs of incisive social criticism in Arniches' theater.

95. *The Rabble (La gentuza);* two acts; November 12, 1913. Music by José Serrano. An energetic defense of lower-class integrity as compared to bourgeois prudery and cunning. Good comedy about popular customs.

96. *The Blue Stone (La piedra azul);* one act; December 15, 1913. Music by R. Calleja. A lyrical sketch apparently based on Edmond About's story, *Le nez d'un notaire* (1862). Humorous but without substance.

97. *The Courtship of Risalia (La corte de Risalia);* two acts; April 11, 1914. Written in collaboration with Antonio Paso. Music by P. Luna. Comic zarzuela regarding a commonplace love conflict.

98. *Friend Melquíades, or The Fish Gets Hooked by its Mouth (El amigo Melquíades, o Por la boca muere el pez);* one act; May 14, 1914. Music by J. Valverde and José Serrano. Two parallel actions involving the loss of honor through deception and its recovery by noble intent. A first-rate sainete about Madrilenean customs.

99. *In the Windmill's Shadow (La sombra del molino);* one act; November 21, 1914. Music by Vicente Arregui. Intrigue in a provincial village. Mediocre zarzuela.

100. *The Priest's Niece (La sobrina del cura);* two acts; December 12, 1914. A small-town priest fights injustice and slander. A good melodrama.

101. *The Adventures of Max and Mino, or How Foolish are the Learned! (Las aventuras de Max y Mino, o ¡Qué tontos son los sabios!);* three parts; December 28, 1914. Written in collaboration with José Jackson Veyán. Music by R. Calleja. Two couples react to a secret formula that heightens or decreases their passion. A somewhat inane comedy.

102. *The Boy from Las Peñuelas, or There's Nothing Worse Than Envy (El chico de Las Peñuelas, o No hay mal como el de la envidia);* one act; May 12, 1915. Music by Rafael Millán. A sainete of strong moral tenor on the theme of envy.

103. *The Quirós Manor (La casa de Quirós);* two acts; November 20, 1915. Rigid conformity with a code of unrealistic values brings parents into conflict with their children. Comic farce of strong social content.

104. *The Star of Olympia (La estrella de Olimpia);* one act; December 23, 1915. Music by R. Calleja. A delightful zarzuela based on Guy de Maupassant's *Boule de Suif* (1880).

105. *Black Coffee (Café solo);* one act; February 18, 1916. Written in collaboration with Joaquín Abati. Street squabbles and domestic misunderstandings. A weak comedietta.

106. *Miss Trevélez (La señorita de Trevélez);* three acts; April 14, 1916. A cruel joke contrived by indolent minds in a provincial town. An artistic masterpiece containing strong moral criticism.

107. *The Conceited and Affected Seraphin, or You Can't Reason About Love (Serafín el Pinturero, o Contra el querer no hay razones);* two acts; May 13, 1916. Written in collaboration with Juan G. Renovales. Music by Foglietti and Roig. Love triumphs over vanity. A shallow sainete.

108. *Petra's Revenge, or One Reaps Where He Has Sown (La venganza de la*

Petra, o Donde las dan, las toman); two acts; April 13, 1917. A loafer
and squanderer mistreats his family until awakened by his daughter's
misfortune.

109. *My Husband's Coming! (¡Que viene mi marido!)*; three acts; March 9,
1918. A cunning swindler's exploitation of a gullible family. Arniches'
first grotesque tragedy.

110. *The Waters of the Manzanares, or The Running River Makes All the
Noise (El agua del Manzanares, o Cuando el río suena. . .)*; one act;
May 4, 1918. Music by Tomás Barrera and Antonio Estremera. A
young girl rejects a suitor for his poverty, seeks out a rich *chulo*, only
to return to her former sweetheart.

111. *The Artificial Woman, or Dr. Miró's Prescription (La mujer artificial,
o La receta del doctor Miró)*; three acts; December 24, 1918. Written
in collaboration with Joaquín Abati. Music by Pablo Luna. Feeble
action and contrived humor keep pace with a weak and fantastic plot.

112. *Trini's Tears (Las lágrimas de la Trini)*; two acts; April 22, 1919.
Written in collaboration with Joaquín Abati. The struggle of a young
girl to find happiness. A melodramatic sainete.

113. *The Flower of the Neighborhood (La flor del barrio)*; two acts; May 30,
1919. A double love conflict involving a fierce mother, a vacillating son,
a wealthy but ugly young lady. A good sainete about Madrilenean
customs.

114. *Great Fortunes (Las grandes fortunas)*; three acts; December 23,
1919. Written in collaboration with Joaquín Abati. A wearisome comic farce concerning the blessings and tribulations of materialism.

115. *The Bosses (Los caciques)*; three acts; February 13, 1920. Sharp
political criticism dealing with the dishonesty and immorality of
public officials. Reminiscent of Nikolai Gogol's *The Inspector General.*

116. *The Count from Lavapiés, or There's No Power Against Cunning (El
conde de Lavapiés, o No hay fuerza contra la astucia)*; two acts; June 22,
1920. Written in collaboration with Alfredo Trigueros Candel. Music
by R. Calleja and Antonio Estremera. A beguiling folk revue of
intrigue in Madrid's slums.

117. *The Sister's Cleverness (La maña de la mañica)*; one act; September
11, 1920 in San Sebastián. Written in collaboration with Joaquín Abati
and Pedro García Marín. A charming sainete of Aragonese customs.

118. *The Forlorn Girl (La chica del gato)*; three acts; April 15, 1921. An
abandoned girl's adventures among a den of thieves. A female
Oliver Twist. Good play.

119. *Frisky Little Mary, or The High Esteem of Merriment (Mariquita la
Pispajo, o No hay bien como la alegría)*; two acts; July 6, 1921. Music
by Antonio Estremera. A girl's expatriate father sends her money,
awakening ambitious schemes in the hearts of her friends. A recasting
of Arniches' own play, *The Rabble* (1913).

120. *The Heroic Town (La heroica villa);* three acts; October 19, 1921. An elegant widow confronts the degenerate world of a hateful and intolerant Spanish town. A piercing social criticism.

121. *That's My Man (Es mi hombre);* three acts; December 22, 1921. A soft-spoken coward acquires true courage when the honor of his daughter is at stake. An outstanding grotesque tragedy and one of Arniches' best plays.

122. *Don't Take Offense, Beatrice (No te ofendas, Beatriz);* three acts; 1921. Written in collaboration with Joaquín Abati. A banal love entanglement inspired by Jacinto Benavente's psychological comedy sketch, *Unintentionally (Sin querer).*

123. *The Look in Her Eyes (El mirar de sus ojos);* one act; 1922. A lovely girl scorns a love-sick lad, runs off with an arrogant suitor, and suffers great unhappiness.

124. *The Fatal Hour (La hora mala);* three acts; May 2, 1922. A betrayed woman seeks suicide but is regenerated by her priest. A conventional melodramatic comedy.

125. *The Tragedy of Marichu (La tragedia de Marichu);* three acts; December, 23, 1922. A woman's psychological readjustment following her husband's infidelity. A good realistic comedy.

126. *Don Juan's Madness (La locura de Don Juan);* three acts; April 5, 1923. A weak-willed father feigns madness in an effort to regain the esteem of his disrespectful family. A well-structured grotesque tragedy.

127. *Sterling Integrity (La dichosa honradez);* three acts; December 22, 1923. Written in collaboration with Antonio Estremera. Grotesque humor pitting the triumph of virtue against the temptations of dishonesty.

128. *Angel Mary (Angela María);* two acts; February 5, 1924. Written in collaboration with Joaquín Abati. A comedy praising the strength and influence of a good woman.

129. *Miracles From the Daily Wage (Los milagros del jornal);* one act; February 23, 1924. Discordant poverty tests the honor of a desperate woman, binding the family together in love and forgiveness. Excellent sainete.

130. *The Road for Everyone (El camino de todos);* three acts; April 4, 1924. Written in collaboration with Antonio Estremera. A jilted man's dismay disappears as he learns the value of faith and hard work.

131. *Juana's Laughter (La risa de Juana);* three acts; October 4, 1924. A girl undertakes the mission of preserving a married couple's happiness. Inspired by Romain Coolus' play, *Petite peste* (1905).

132. *The Embittered Quintin, or He Who Sows the Wind . . . (Don Quintín el amargao, o El que siembra vientos . . .);* two acts; November 26, 1924. Written in collaboration with Antonio Estremera. A moral sainete on the themes of irascibility and artifice.

133. *Fragrant Little Roses (Rositas de olor);* three acts; December 23, 1924. An orphan and her friend are protected by a childless old couple. A good melodramatic sainete.

134. *The Master Stonecutters (Los maestros canteros);* two acts; 1924. Written in collaboration with Antonio Estremera. An unpublished sainete.

135. *Uncle Quico (El tío Quico);* three acts; March 28, 1925. Written in collaboration with J. Aguilar Catena. A rural comedy combining folk scenes with melodrama.

136. *What a Charming Fellow! (¡Qué hombre tan simpático!);* three acts; June 5, 1925. Written in collaboration with Antonio Paso and Antonio Estremera. A banal comedy about chicanery disguised as charm.

137. *Trini's Blunder, or Under an Evil Cloak (El tropiezo de la Trini, o Bajo una mal capa);* two acts; October 29, 1925. Written in collaboration with Antonio Estremera. The fast, funny, and pathetic actions of a gullible young lady.

138. *Goodbye, Beatrice (Adiós, Beatriz);* three acts; November 6, 1925. Written in collaboration with Emilio Sáez. Farcical humor centered around the bonds of love.

139. *Pepita's Cross (La cruz de Pepita);* three acts; December 23, 1925. A conflict of interests between a kindhearted woman and her ugly, irascible sister. Inferior comedy.

140. *Serene Master Pepe, or The Blackberry Stain (El señor Pepe el templao, o La mancha de la mora);* two acts; December 23, 1925. Written in collaboration with Antonio Estremera. Music by Cayo Vela. Misjudgment of character occasions complicated dispute.

141. *What a Charming Woman! (¡Qué encanto de mujer!);* three acts; December 24, 1925. Written in collaboration with Antonio Paso. A threadbare comedy based on Verneuil's *My Varsovian Cousin (Mi prima de Varsovia).*

142. *I am Dying of Jealousy (Los celos me están matando);* three acts; April 2, 1926. Written in collaboration with Antonio Paso and Antonio Estremera. A farcical tragicomedy on the pains of love. Lacks a clear tragic undertone.

143. *I Was Born in Aragon (En Aragón hi nació);* three acts; September 21, 1926. Written in collaboration with Pedro García Marín. A comedy of light humor stressing Aragonese customs.

144. *The Last Monkey, or The Lad from the Store (El último mono, o El chico de la tienda);* three acts; November 10, 1926. A poor and seemingly stupid boy discovers the treachery of a friend. Weakness triumphs over evil's strength.

145. *Gracious, How Handsome I am! (¡Mechachis, qué guapo soy!);* three acts; December 18, 1926. A candid attack on the degenerate moneyed ignorant who place a financial value on love and marriage.

146. *My Mother Married Me Off, or Elena's Fickle Concerns (Me caso mi madre, o Las veleidades de Elena);* three acts; November 18, 1927. A technically fine comedy based on a French play by Emilio Berr and reminiscent of *The Crazy Adventure (La loca aventura)* by José Juan Cadenas (1915).

147. *Mr. Adrian the Dupe, or How Tough It Is To Be Good (El señor Adrián el primo o Qué malo es ser bueno);* three acts; December 21, 1927. Pursuing good for its own sake, the hero is accosted by evil forces. A good comedy of high moral tone.

148. *Mediacapa's Lineage (El solar de Mediacapa);* three acts; December 21, 1928. An arrogant and cynical Don Juan type meets his match in a woman lacking moral scruples. Good tragicomedy.

149. *The Wolf's Hide (La piel del lobo);* June, 1928. Unpublished comedy.

150. *Model Jail, or The Villain's Revenge (La cárcel Modelo, o La venganza de un malvado);* three acts; January 29, 1929. Written in collaboration with Joaquín Abati. A criminal plots and implements his vengeance. Insubstantial comedy.

151. *Night Patrol Song (Coplas de ronda);* three acts; April 12, 1929. Written in collaboration with José de Lucio. Music by Francisco Alonso. A lengthy zarzuela that features sprightly lyrics over dramatic action.

152. *The World Is All Yours (Para ti es el mundo);* three acts; October 17, 1929. A wealthy widow indulges to excess her only son. Good comic farce.

153. *The Countess is Sad (La condesa está triste);* three acts; January 24, 1930. A wealthy widow discovers that the young man she loves is a fraud. Grotesque tragedy censuring hypocrisy among the pseudo-aristocratic.

154. *The Junk Collectors (Los chamerileros);* three acts; 1930 in Barcelona. Written in collaboration with Joaquín Abati and José de Lucio. Unpublished farce.

155. *Mister Badanas (El señor Badanas);* three acts; December 19, 1930. Feigning obduracy, a timid nobody rises to high distinction. Very good tragicomedy.

156. *Living on Dreams (Vivir de ilusiones);* three acts; November 12, 1931. The tragedy of a highborn but impoverished widow yearning for the return of her peerage and hoping to marry her daughter to a nobleman.

157. *The Goddess Laughs (La diosa ríe);* three acts; December 31, 1931. A humble clerk's passion for a famous stage actress. Heartache and humor blend well in this grotesque tragedy.

158. *The Happy Women (Las dichosas faldas);* three acts; January 25, 1933. A young, strong, and persevering wife discovers her weak husband's infidelity. Wearisome domestic conflict.

159. *Look Out for Love! (¡Cuidado con el amor!)*; three acts; March 4, 1933. A case history of the contrasting behavior and attitudes of two couples, from engagement through marriage. Upper-class socio-critical setting.

160. *Twelve O'Clock High (Las doce en punto)*; three acts; December 21, 1933. A father's pathological obsession for punctuality threatens disruption of family union.

161. *Chaste Don José (El casto don José)*; three acts; December 23, 1933. A grotesque tragedy of playful banter concerning a very proper bachelor's emotional upheaval when he falls in love.

162. *The Sins of the World (Peccata mundi)*; 1934. Written in collaboration with Antonio Estremera. Music by Jacinto Guerrero. Unpublished musical revue.

163. *Good Health and Prosperity (Salud y pesetas)*; 1934. Written in collaboration with Joaquín Abati and José de Lucio. Unpublished grotesque farce.

164. *Portillo's Woman Paquita (Paquita, la del Portillo)*; one act; October, 1934. Written in collaboration with Antonio Estremera. An unpublished zarzuela.

165. *The Nincompoop's Tragedy (La tragedia del pelele)*; three acts; April 9, 1935. The bittersweet history of an abulic man and those who exploit his lack of will power. A good farce.

166. *I Want To (Yo Quiero)*; three acts; January 14, 1936. The adventures of a poor boy who advocates the merit of doing good deeds.

167. *It Suits Your Interests, So Kiss Me (Bésame, que te conviene)*; April 11, 1936. Written in collaboration with Antonio Estremera. Unpublished comedy.

168. *Father Pitillo (El Padre Pitillo)*; three acts; April 9, 1937 in Buenos Aires; October 6, 1939 in Madrid. A just priest risks the loss of his office by defending an ill-used girl from slander.

169. *The Sleeping Beast (La fiera dormida)*; three acts; March, 1939 in Buenos Aires; November 10, 1943 posthumously in Madrid. A melodramatic comedy of love, pain, and gaiety.

170. *That Fellow Miseria (El tío Miseria)*; three acts; May 18, 1938 in Buenos Aires; December 15, 1940 in Barcelona. A well-devised melodrama on the classical theme of the miser and supporting a thesis on the supremacy of love.

171. *The Little Man (El hombrecillo)*; three acts; December 10, 1941 in Barcelona. The power of love enables a hunchback to rise above his deformity while the value of work endears their land to a group of peasants. A tragicomedy in a rural setting.

172. *You Already Know Paquita (Ya conoces a Paquita)*; three acts; July 10, 1942 in Pamplona. Conflict between a wife's voluble but virtuous character and her husband's lack of trust.

173. *Don Verdades;* three acts; October 27, 1943, posthumously. A man's loyalty to truth in conflict with his rationalized concession to a lie. Arniches' last written work. Excellent depiction of a true tragicomic figure.

Other plays (unpublished) attributed to Carlos Arniches:

174. *The Madcap Princess (La princesa tarambana);* date unknown.
175. *The Great Courtiers (Las grandes cortesanas);* 1902.
176. *The Eternal Romance (El eterno romance);* 1908.
177. *Gentlemen . . . Do Something Else (Señoritos . . . , a otra cosa);* 1934.
178. *Men That Weep (Los hombres que lloran);* 1934.
179. *The Mirror for Large Men (Espejo de grandes);* June 11, 1946, posthumously. Comedy.

Other writings:

Reading Primer (Cartilla y cuaderno de lectura); 1887. Brief compendium of Alfonso XII's reign.
From the Soul of Madrid (Del Madrid castizo); 1917. Contains eleven one-act sainetes with intriguing moral and social theses. The collection includes *The Paupers (Los pobres); The Guilty (Los culpables); Nicanor's Prize, or To Whom Shall I Reward the Raffle? (El premio de Nicanor, o ¿A quién le doy la suerte?); The Neutrals (Los neutrales); The Philosophic Cobbler, or Another Year, Another Chance (El zapatero filósofo, o Año nuevo, vida nueva); The Impassioned (Los pasionales); The Laughter of the People (La risa del pueblo); The Scientific Couple (La pareja científica); The Atheists (Los ateos); The Wealthy (Los ricos); The Ambitious (Los ambiciosos).*
Blessed San Isidro! (¡San Isidro bendito!); May, 1934. One-act rapid sainete. Thematically similar to *The Stars.*
Many articles, lectures, letters, and reminiscences were published by Arniches throughout his lifetime in different periodicals.

Index

146